Editor
Eric Migliaccio

Managing Editor
Ina Massler Levin, M.A.

Illustrator
Clint McKnight

Cover Artist
Brenda DiAntonis

Art Production Manager
Kevin Barnes

ArtCoordinator
Renée Christine Yates

Imaging
James Edward Grace

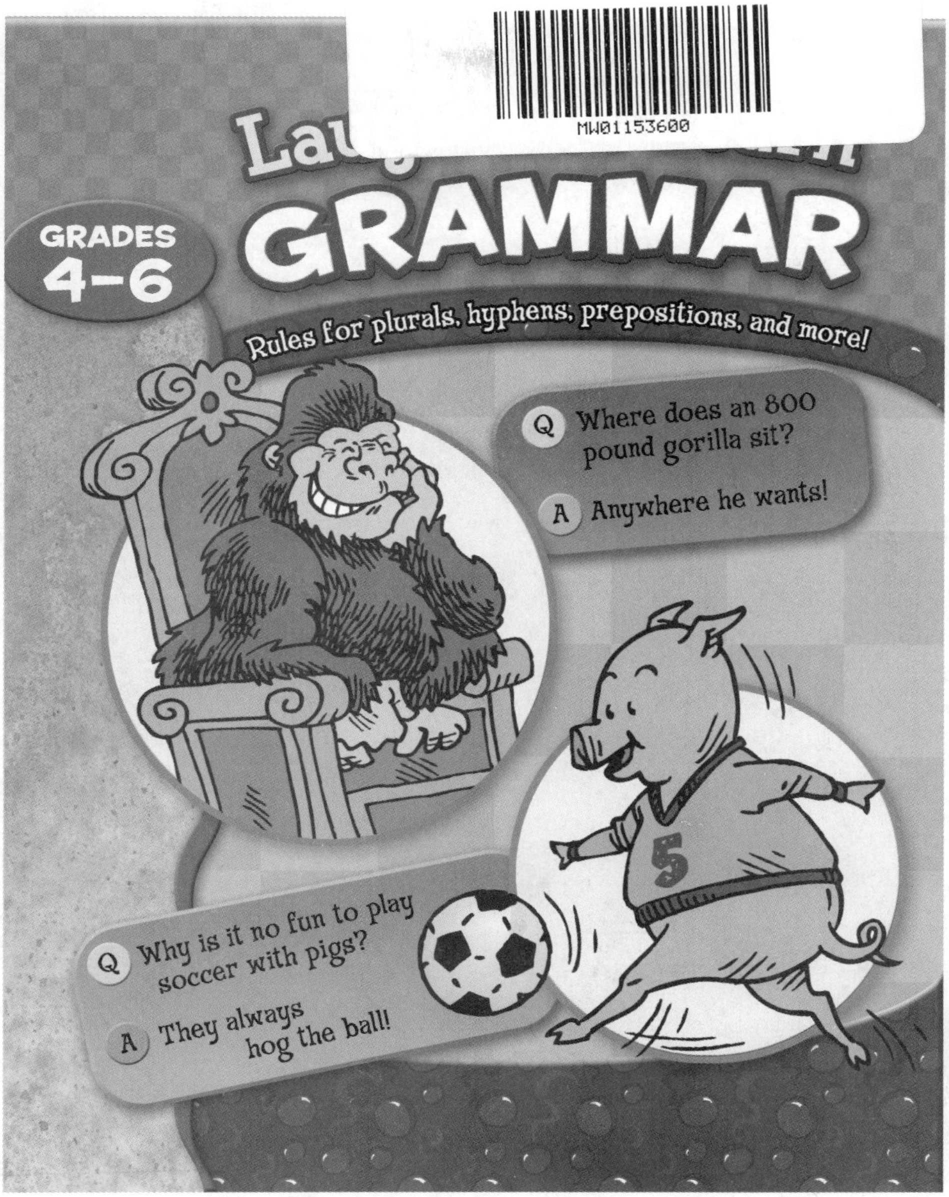

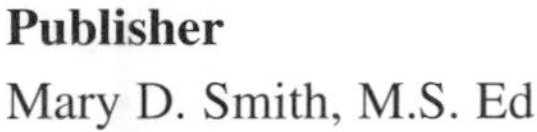

Publisher
Mary D. Smith, M.S. Ed.

GRADES 4–6

GRAMMAR

Rules for plurals, hyphens, prepositions, and more!

Q Where does an 800 pound gorilla sit?
A Anywhere he wants!

Q Why is it no fun to play soccer with pigs?
A They always hog the ball!

Author

Debra J. Housel, M.S. Ed.

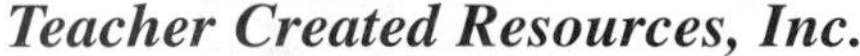

Teacher Created Resources, Inc.
6421 Industry Way
Westminster, CA 92683
www.teachercreated.com
ISBN-1-4206-3019-9

Table of Contents

Introduction

Everyone enjoys a good laugh, and children are no exception. Even preschoolers can listen to and enjoy a joke based on an obvious incongruity. *Laugh and Learn Grammar* capitalizes on your students' natural interest in word play by providing grammar and usage examples and practice exclusively through jokes and riddles.

Researchers believe that humor development parallels Piaget's stages of cognitive development. Just as physical play strengthens children's bodies, word play develops their minds. To understand humor, students must learn new things about words or logical relationships. Students in the middle grades and English-language learners of all ages expand their senses of humor as they realize that the meaning of words can be ambiguous and that words and phrases may sound alike yet have different connotations. Thus, jokes and riddles stimulate intellectual growth.

Many children enjoy learning and telling jokes and riddles. If the jokes and riddles are simply memorized and repeated, this won't necessarily improve their language skills. However, *Laugh and Learn Grammar* strengthens students' minds by making them think about the language structure of the joke. At an age where jokes and riddles are motivational, *Laugh and Learn Grammar* will appeal to your students in a way that no other grammar and usage exercises can.

Research shows that what's most important is that a joke requires the optimal amount of effort. Moderately challenging jokes are seen as the funniest. Students view as babyish those that are too easy or obvious. Yet if a joke is too difficult, students tire of trying to figure it out, or worse, feel foolish because they can't grasp the meaning. These factors have been carefully considered in the selection of jokes and riddles used in *Laugh and Learn Grammar.*

How to Use This Book

Use this book as a supplement to your English grammar and usage instruction. After teaching a topic, make an overhead transparency of the related lesson page from *Laugh and Learn Grammar.* Display it and discuss it with your students. Each lesson page is followed by at least one practice page for your students to complete independently. Extra practice pages are provided for topics for which students frequently need reinforcement.

Encourage your students to tell the jokes they learn with their family members. By sharing the jokes orally, your students will revisit the language concepts that they reinforce. You can encourage this by having your students take home the practice page overnight and submit it the next day with the number of the joke or riddle that "went over the best" circled.

A Note About Verbs: In this book, verbs that end in *-ing* are classified as continuous action verbs (see pages 31 and 32). This term comes from *Verbs in Action*, a book written for English-language learners by Linda Ferreire. Ferreire labels verbs ending in *-ing* as present continuous, past continuous, and future continuous.

Nouns • • • • • • • • • • • • Rules to Remember

***Rule:* A noun is a person, place, or thing.**

What did the rabbits say when the farmer caught them in his garden?
. . . "Lettuce alone!"

What travels around the world without ever leaving its corner?
. . . a stamp

What starts with "t," ends with "t," and is full of "t"?
. . . a teapot

***Rule:* A noun is often the subject of a sentence. It takes action.**

Girl: "Magicians always score well on tests."
Boy: "Why is that?"
Girl: "They're great at trick questions."

- *Explanation: The noun (Magicians) takes the action (score).*

Boy: "My little brother planted pennies in our backyard."
Girl: "Why?"
Boy: "He wanted to raise some cash."

- *Explanation: The brother planted.*

***Rule:* A noun can also be an object in a sentence. This means that it receives action (has something done to it).**

Why did the lawyer leave the courtroom in his underwear?
. . . He'd lost his lawsuit.

- *Explanation: The courtroom was left.*

Girl: "The chimpanzee escaped from his cage at the zoo."
Boy: "How?"
Girl: "He used a monkey wrench."

- *Explanation: The cage was escaped from.*

***Rule:* A noun can also be a concept such as love, freedom, peace, etc.**

Where can you always find peace, love, and understanding?
. . . in the dictionary

Nouns • • • • • • • • • • • • • • • • Practice Page

Directions: Fill in the missing noun to complete each joke.

---

1. What's really at the end of the rainbow?
   . . . the ________________________ "W"

2. Boy at the bus stop: "When does the bus stop here?"
   . . . "Whenever the bus ________________________ steps on the brakes."

3. What does a spider bride wear when she gets married?
   . . . a webbing ________________________

4. How are snow and rain like bedding?
   . . . ________________________ blankets the ground, and
   ________________________ comes down in sheets

5. Student: "Would you punish me for something I didn't do?"
   Teacher: "No, of course not."
   Student: "Good, because I didn't do my ________________________."

6. Traveler: "I'd like to buy a round-trip ________________________ to Los Angeles."
   Ticket agent: "Sorry, but all of our tickets are rectangular."

7. What happened to the ________________________ who ate cookies in bed before going to sleep?
   . . . He had a crummy night's sleep.

8. Girl: "Why have you started avoiding Rose?"
   Boy: "My ________________________ told me that I'm allergic to flowers."

9. Boy: "I lost my dog."
   Girl: "Then put up signs around your ________________________."
   Boy: "That's ridiculous, my dog can't read."

10. Girl: "The United ________________________ is founded on the ideals of liberty and justice for all people."
    Boy: "One of those reminds me of the North Pole."
    Girl: "Which one?"
    Boy: "Just-ice."

Proper Nouns • • • • • • • • Rules to Remember

Rule: **Capitalize the first letter of any proper noun. A proper noun is the name of a specific person, place, or thing.**

Why didn't George Washington ever need a bed?
. . . because he could not lie

Boy: "What's the capital of Alaska?"
Girl: "Juneau."
Boy: "Of course I know, but I'm asking you!"

Where did Abraham Lincoln write the Gettysburg Address?
. . . on an envelope, of course

Rule: **Capitalize the names of months, days of the week, and holidays.**

If April showers bring May flowers, what do May flowers bring?
. . . Pilgrims

Which are the two strongest days of the seven?
. . . Saturday and Sunday . . . the others are weekdays

Boy: "Why was your January math grade so low?"
Girl: "Everything is always marked down after Christmas."

Rule: **Capitalize the names of languages, nationalities, events, and time periods.**

Why did the British get so mad about the Boston Tea Party?
. . . They weren't invited.

Why are the Middle Ages also called the Dark Ages?
. . . because there were so many knights.

Rule: **Acronyms are nouns made of the first letters of words. Acronyms are written in solid capital letters and are usually pronounced by their individual letters.**

How did the dog stop the DVD player?
. . . It pressed the paws button.

- *Explanation: "DVD" is the acronym for "digital video disc."*

Proper Nouns • • • • • • • • • • Practice Page

Directions: Complete each joke by writing a proper noun. Remember to capitalize when necessary. Use the hints in parentheses to help you.

1. Where do ghosts and goblins go swimming?
   . . . in ________________________ Erie
   (Hint: *one of the Great Lakes)*

2. Who is never hungry on ________________________?
   . . . The turkey, because it's stuffed.
   (Hint: *holiday)*

3. Why are fish terrified of computers?
   . . . They don't want to get caught in the ________________.
   (Hint: *another name for the World Wide Web)*

4. Girl: "I'm glad I wasn't born in Italy."
   Boy: "Why is that?"
   Girl: "I don't know how to speak ________________________."
   (Hint: *a language)*

5. In which month do people talk the least?
   . . . ________________________, because it's the shortest month.
   (Hint: *a month)*

6. Where are chili beans grown?
   . . . at the ________________________
   (Hint: *the point farthest north on Earth)*

7. Where does Friday come before ________________?
   . . . in the dictionary
   (Hint: *the day in the middle of the week)*

8. Where do mummies go for vacation?
   . . . to the ________________________ Sea
   (Hint: *word that means the opposite of "living")*

9. Why did ________________________ have too few reindeer
   on ________________ Eve?
   . . . Comet stayed home to clean the sink.
   (Hint: *a famous gift giver's name and a holiday)*

10. Why did the rock star hit his ________________________ with a hammer?
    . . . He wanted a smash hit.
    (Hint: *the acronym for "compact disc")*

Proper Nouns • • • • • • • • • • More Practice

Directions: Complete each joke by writing a proper noun. Remember to capitalize when necessary. Use the hints in parentheses to help you.

1. Why was ______________________ a poor football player?

   . . . Her coach was a pumpkin.

   ***(Hint:** rags-to-riches princess with the glass slipper)*

2. Why couldn't the worms enter ______________________ 's ark in an apple?

   . . . They had to go in pairs.

   ***(Hint:** Biblical ark builder)*

3. Boy: "How many seconds are in a year?"

   Girl: "I have no idea. How many?"

   Boy: "Twelve. __________________ second, __________________ second, ..."

   ***(Hint:** first month of the year and second month of the year)*

4. Why did _______________ _______________ have a great fall?

   . . . to make up for a lousy summer

   ***(Hint:** nursery rhyme character's name)*

5. Where do ants come from?

   . . . ______________________

   ***(Hint:** continent at the bottom of the globe)*

6. What do the miners look for in ___________________?

   . . . cold gold

   ***(Hint:** U.S. state farthest north)*

7. What has four eyes but can't see a thing?

   . . . the ______________________ River

   ***(Hint:** name of the longest river in the U.S.)*

8. What did the _____________________ reporter say during the weather forecast?

   . . . "Chili today, hot tamale."

   ***(Hint:** nationality of a person living in a nation that shares a border with the U.S.)*

9. Why didn't the acrobat get money from the ______________________?

   . . . He had to keep his balance.

   ***(Hint:** the acronym for automatic teller machine)*

10. What would you get if you dropped a banana from the top of the _______________ State Building?

    . . . a banana split

    ***(Hint:** famous skyscraper in New York City)*

Plurals • • • • • • • • • • • • • Rules to Remember

Rule: **To show more than one of a noun, make it plural by adding the letter *s* to the end of the noun.**

Student: "I ain't got a pencil."
Teacher: "Don't say 'ain't'! It's, 'I don't have a pencil; you don't have a pencil; they don't have a pencil.'"
Student: "Gosh, where did all the pencils go?"

• *Explanation: The plural of "pencil" is "pencils."*

Little boy: "Daddy, will you put on my shoes?"
Father: "I can't. They won't fit me."

• *Explanation: The plural of "shoe" is "shoes."*

Rule: **When a noun ends in *s, x, z, sh,* or *ch,* add the letters *es* to the end to form the plural.**

Why can't anyone's nose be 12 inches long?
. . . because then it would be a foot

• *Explanation: The plural of "inch" is "inches."*

What kind of guitars do octopuses play?
. . . eel-ectric guitars

• *Explanation: The plural of "octopus" is "octopuses."*

Rule: **When a noun ends in a consonant + *y*, change the *y* to *i* and add the letters *es* to form the plural.**

What sort of music do bunnies like best?
. . . hip hop

• *Explanation: The plural of "bunny" is "bunnies."*

What kind of fruit do scarecrows like?
. . . strawberries

• *Explanation: The plural of "strawberry" is "strawberries."*

Rule: **When a noun ends with an *f* or *fe*, drop the f and add *ves* to form the plural.**

What do calves like to have read to them?
. . . dairy tales

• *Explanation: The plural of "calf" is "calves."*

Why did the elves ask the turkey to join their band?
. . . He was the only one who had drumsticks.

• *Explanation: The plural of "elf" is "elves."*

Plurals • • • • • • • • • • • • • Practice Page

Directions: Complete each joke by writing the plural of the noun(s) given in parentheses.

1. Why is a dairy barn so noisy?
   . . . The cows have ________________________. *(horn)*

2. What's the tallest building in any city?
   . . . The library, because it has the most ________________________. (*story*)

3. How are playing cards like ________________________? (*wolf*)
   . . . Both come in packs.

4. How did the farmer mend the torn knees in his pants?
   . . . with cabbage ________________________ (*patch*)

5. What three things can you find in July but never in August?
   . . . the ________________________ J, L, and Y (*letter*)

6. Why was the baby ant so confused?
   . . . All of its ________________________ were ________________________. (*uncle, ant*)

7. What has ________________________ without ________________________,
   ________________________ without ________________________, and
   ________________________ without water? (*city, building, forest, tree, river*)
   . . . a map

8. Why are tooth ________________________ so intelligent? (fairy)
   . . . They collect a lot of wisdom teeth.

9. What do ________________________ put on their hair? (*witch*)
   . . . scare spray

10. How do you stop a herd of ________________________ from charging? (*rhinoceros*)
    . . . Take away their credit cards.

Unusual Plurals • • • • • • Rules to Remember

Rule: **Some common words form their plurals in unusual ways. These have to be memorized.**

Mom: "You have your shoes on the wrong feet."
Son: "No, I don't. These are the only feet I have."

- *Explanation: The plural of "foot" is "feet."*

What does a cat call mice that wear rollerskates?
. . . meals on wheels

- *Explanation: The plural of "mouse" is "mice."*

What has 100 teeth but no mouth?
. . . a saw

- *Explanation: The plural of "tooth" is "teeth."*

What makes men mean?
. . . the letter A

- *Explanation: The plural of "man" is "men."*

While their parents work, where do ghost children go for the day?
. . . to a dayscare center

- *Explanation: The plural of "child" is "children."*

Why didn't the police catch the women who robbed the laundromat?
. . . They made a clean getaway.

- *Explanation: The plural of "woman" is "women."*

What did the baby sardine say when he saw a submarine?
"Look, Mom, a can of people!"

- *Explanation: The plural of "person" is "people."*

Which birds are the most like a car?
. . . Geese . . . because they honk!

- *Explanation: The plural of "goose" is "geese."*

Rule: **A few nouns do not have a plural form. They stay the same for both singular and plural.**

Why did the man capture 100 deer?
. . . He wanted 100 bucks.

What do sea monsters eat for dinner?
. . . fish and ships

Why did the man carry his 12 sheep across his frozen pond?
. . . He didn't want anyone pulling the wool over his ice!

Unusual Plurals • • • • • • • • • Practice Page

Directions: To complete each joke, fill in the unusual plural for each noun in parentheses.

1. Why are ________________________ so well educated? (*fish*)
   . . . They live in schools.

2. What has three ________________________
   but can't stand? (*foot*)
   . . . a yardstick

3. What gets the biggest laugh from the
   ________________________ who enjoy it the least? (*person*)
   . . . being tickled

4. What has ________________________ but never eats? (*tooth*)
   . . . a zipper

5. What is it that little ________________________ spend a lot of time making, yet no one ever sees? (*child*)
   . . . noise

6. How are ________________________ like icicles? (*goose*)
   . . . They both grow down.

7. Boy: "This morning my uncle shot two ____________________ in his pajamas." (*deer*)
   Girl: "How did the ______________________ get into your uncle's pajamas?" (*deer*)

8. How did ________________________ make wooden tools? (*caveman*)
   . . . a whittle at a time

9. What ________________________ make the best bookkeepers? (*woman*)
   . . . The ones who never return the books you lent them.

10. Boy: "Have you ever seen the Catskill Mountains?"
    Girl: "No, but I've seen them kill ________________________." (*mouse*)

Possessive Nouns • • • • • Rules to Remember

Rule: **To show ownership (possession), add an apostrophe *s* to the end of the noun.**

What do you call a beekeeper's income?
. . . honey money

- *Explanation: The beekeeper owns the income.*

Girl: "I have my dad's nose and my mom's ears."
Boy: "Gosh, they must look strange without them."

- *Explanation: The dad owns the nose; the mom owns the ears.*

What's the world's largest jewel?
. . . a baseball diamond

- *Explanation: The world owns the jewel.*

Rule: **Usually a noun follows the possessive, except when the owned item is implied.**

Why did the Dalmatian go to the cleaner's?
. . . His coat had spots.

- *Explanation: It's implied that the cleaner owns a business.*

What candles burn longer. . . the ones on a boy's birthday cake or the ones on a girl's?
. . . No candles burn longer. . . all candles burn shorter!

- *Explanation: It's implied that the girl and the boy own birthday cakes.*

Rule: **To show ownership when the noun is plural and ends in *s*, add an apostrophe to the end of the plural noun.**

What's the most suitable fabric pattern for bank executives' clothing?
. . . checks

Boy: "A waiter from my parents' restaurant is taking me canoeing."
Girl: "Well, I wouldn't go canoeing with him."
Boy: "Why not?"
Girl: "He will think tipping is a good idea."

Rule: **To show ownership when the noun is a plural that doesn't end in *s*, add an *'s*.**

Why aren't chickens welcome in most people's homes?
. . . They use fowl language!

Possessive Nouns • • • • • • • Practice Page

Directions: Finish each joke by making the noun in parentheses into a possessive. Remember that with plurals, you add only an apostrophe.

---

1. Which Revolutionary War hero always slept with his shoes on?
   . . . ______________________ horse (*Paul Revere*)

2. Why did the farmer plant the ______________________ eggs? (*chickens*)
   . . . He wanted to grow eggplants.

3. What do you call a ______________________ baseball glove? (*girl*)
   . . . a hermit

4. What is a ______________________ favorite holiday? (*vampire*)
   . . . Fangsgiving

5. What is most ______________________ favorite fruit? (*teenagers*)
   . . . dates

6. Son: "I've been invited to ______________________ birthday party, but I can't go." (*Jamie*)
   Dad: "Why not?"
   Son: "It says from four to seven, and I'm 11."

7. Girl: "Is it really true that you and your dad used to be lion tamers?"
   Boy: "Yes."
   Girl: "And you actually put your head into the ______________________ mouths?" (*lions*)
   Boy: "Yes, but I only did it to look for my dad."

8. Teacher: "What is net profit?"
   Student: "A ______________________ earnings." (*fisherman*)

9. What is the ______________________ most dangerous flower? (*world*)
   . . . a snapdragon

10. Tutor: "If you had $36 in one pocket and $59 in another, what would you have?"
    Student: "Somebody ______________________ clothes." (*else*)

Personal Pronouns • • • • Rules to Remember

Personal pronouns take the place of specific nouns.

Rule: **A subject of a sentence takes action. (As the subject of a sentence, use these personal pronouns: *I, we, they, she,* or *he.*)**

Boy: "My best friend and I used to enjoy doing newspaper puzzles together."
Girl: "So what happened?"
Boy: "We ended with cross words."

What do dragons do on the weekends?
. . . They let off steam.

Why did the coach throw Cinderella off the basketball team?
. . . She ran away from the ball.

How did the barber-turned-criminal escape from the police officers that chased him?
. . . He knew plenty of short cuts.

Rule: **Personal pronouns can also act as objects. (Remember that an object receives action. As objects, use these personal pronouns: *me, us, them, her,* or *him.*)**

Sergeant: "Soldier, your rifle is your best friend. You work together as a team."
Private: "I know that, Sarge, so please don't ask me to fire him."

Girl: "My cousin flew here to visit me."
Boy: "Did you meet her at the airport?"
Girl: "No, I've known her all my life."

Why doesn't an apple tree have pears?
. . . It can't bear them.

Rule: **Two personal pronouns can act as subjects or objects: *you* and *it.***

What do you break with a whisper instead of a hammer?
. . . a secret

How many feet are in a yard?
. . . It depends on how many people are standing in it.

• *Explanation: "It" serves as both the subject and the object in this sentence.*

Personal Pronouns • • • • • • Practice Page

Directions: Finish each punchline using the appropriate personal pronoun(s) from the box. The words may be used more than once. Remember to capitalize a pronoun that begins a sentence.

it	I	me	she	he	him	they	them	we	us

1. Why are frogs so happy?
   . . . ___________ eat whatever bugs ___________.

2. What did the mirror do when the boy told it a funny joke?
   . . . ___________ cracked up.

3. Why did the girl eat 1,000 fortune cookies?
   . . . ___________ wanted to become wealthy.

4. Why did the boy bring home lots of steel wool?
   . . . ___________ wanted his mom to knit ___________ a car.

5. Do you like home cooking?
   . . . ___________ don't know; ___________ have never tasted a home.

6. What did the dime say to the quarter?
   . . . "It would make more cents if ___________ went together."

7. Girl: "___________ know a restaurant where we can eat dirt cheap."
   Boy: "But ___________ don't want to eat dirt!"

8. What did the cat cry out when the dog grabbed its tail?
   . . . "That's the end of ___________!"

9. What did the cucumber say to the vinegar?
   . . . "Well this is a fine pickle you've gotten ___________ into!"

10. Why did Santa Claus plant a gigantic garden?
    . . . ___________ likes to hoe, hoe, hoe!

Possessive Pronouns • • • Rules to Remember

Possessive case pronouns show ownership. It's much like a possessive noun, except that you never use an apostrophe with a pronoun.

Rule: **The pronouns underlined in these jokes show ownership.**

Dad in pet store: "I'd like to get a dog for my daughter."
Pet store owner: "I'm sorry, sir, but I don't do exchanges."

Woman: "I'd like to try on that red dress in your store window."
Store clerk: "We'd prefer if you used a dressing room."

Where does a polar bear keep its money?
. . . in a snowbank

What is the only nail a carpenter hates to hit with his hammer?
. . . his fingernail

Boy: "How can I make antifreeze?"
Girl: "Hide her flannel nightgown."

How do evergreen trees keep their needles so neat?
. . . They use pine combs.

Boy: "Our school is haunted."
Girl: "What makes you say that?"
Boy: "Everyone keeps talking about our school spirit."

What did the bee write on a valentine for his sweetheart?
. . . Honey, bee mine.

Possessive Pronouns • • • • • Practice Page

Directions: Complete each joke by filling in a possessive case pronoun from the box. Two of the words are used more than once.

their	your	our	its	mine	my	his	her

1. When does a clock stop working?
   . . . when ________________________ time is up
2. Why do mother kangaroos hate rainy days?
   . . . because then ________________________ kids have to play inside
3. What did the ground say to the rain?
   . . . "Great! You've made ________________________ name mud!"
4. Lady: "Do you have any kittens going cheap?"
   Pet store clerk: "No, all of ________________________ kittens go "meow.""
5. What's the best thing you can put into a dessert?
   . . . ________________________ teeth!
6. Where do spirits pick up __________________ mail?
   . . . at the ghost office.
7. Why did the father put sunscreen on ________________ little boy?
   . . . He wanted to prevent son burn.
8. Man: "Is this your baseball?"
   Boy shrugs, but says nothing.
   Man: "Somebody just hit this ball through my garage window."
   Boy: "Well, then it's not ________________________."
9. Why did the mother bat hate the letter R?
   . . . It turned ________________________ baby into a brat!
10. What would you do if you found a $50 bill in ____________________ pants pocket?
    . . . I'd wonder whose pants I had on.

Reflexive Pronouns • • • Rules to R

Refl

***Rule:* Reflexive pronouns are compound words ending with *self*. They are used to refe mentioned people or animals.**

Doctor: "You can swim, dive, and water ski while wearing this n . kind of bandage."

Injured person: "Wow, that's terrific! I couldn't do any of those things before I hurt myself."

• *Explanation: "myself" refers back to "I."*

How did the carpenter fall off the 100-foot-tall ladder without injuring himself?

. . . He fell off the first step.

• *Explanation: "himself" refers back to the carpenter.*

Why should astronauts wear bulletproof vests?

. . . to protect themselves from shooting stars

• *Explanation: "themselves" refers back to "astronauts."*

Why does a dog scratch itself?

. . . It's the only one who knows where it itches.

• *Explanation: "itself" refers back to the dog.*

***Rule:* The reflexive pronouns *itself* and *themselves* can refer to nonliving things.**

Why can't a bike stand up by itself without a kickstand?

. . . because it's two-tired

• *Explanation: "itself" refers back to the bike.*

Bill collector: "Better Windows installed energy-efficient windows in your home 13 months ago but still hasn't received a single payment from you."

Customer: "But the salesperson said that those windows would pay for themselves in 12 months!"

• *Explanation: "themselves" refers back to the windows.*

exive Pronouns • • • • • • Practice Page

Directions: Choose the reflexive pronoun from the box to complete each joke. One of the words is used twice.

itself	myself	yourself	herself	himself	themselves	ourselves

1. When did the raspberry finally decide that it needed help?

   . . . when it found ______________________ in a jam

2. Judge: "You've been charged with five crimes in the past two years. What do you have to say for ______________________?"

   Defendant: "Nobody's perfect."

3. Why did the rabbit build ______________________ a house?

   . . . She was fed up with the hole thing.

4. Customer: "Can I put this wallpaper on ______________________?"

   Clerk: "Sure, but it would look a lot better on the wall."

5. What do rock stars do if they catch ______________________ on fire?

   . . . Stop, rock, and roll.

6. Why did the man call ____________ an experienced actor?

   . . . He had broken his leg and was in a cast for six months.

7. Boy: "Have you ever seen a catfish?"

   Girl: "Yes."

   Boy: "How did it hold the pole by ____________________?"

8. Teacher: "Where is your homework?"

   Student: "It's not here because it served a life-saving mission."

   Teacher: "What?!"

   Student: "Last night our furnace broke, so we burned my homework to keep ____________________ from freezing to death."

Indefinite Pronouns • • • Rules to Remember

Indefinite pronouns refer to unnamed or unknown people or things. They take the place of nouns and can serve as the subject of a sentence.

Rule: **Compound words beginning with *any* are indefinite pronouns.**

Which animal is the most generous?
. . . the skunk . . . it'll give anybody a scent.

What keys can't fit anyone's door lock?
. . . the Florida Keys

Which vegetable has eyes but can't see anything?
. . . a potato

Where does an 800-pound gorilla sit?
. . . Anywhere it wants to!

Rule: **Compound words beginning with *every* are indefinite pronouns.**

Why do fences often surround cemeteries?
. . . because everybody is dying to get in

Girl: "Guess who I saw yesterday!"
Boy: "Everyone you looked at."
How does a rooster keep his feathers so nicely groomed?
. . . He carries his comb everywhere he goes.

Rule: **Compound words beginning with *no* are indefinite pronouns.**

Why is it so hard to find a store that sells alligator shoes?
. . . Nobody wants to wait on alligators.

What's the most elusive thing in the world?
. . . A shadow. No one has ever caught one.

• *Note: "no one" is always two words.*

Girl: "My dog can do math."
Boy: "How do you know that?"
Girl: "When I asked him what two minus two was, he said nothing."

Rule: **Compound words beginning with *some* are indefinite pronouns.**

What is a lumberjack?
. . . Something used to lift up a flat tree.

Indefinite Pronouns • • • • • • Practice Page

Directions: Use the pronouns in the box to complete these jokes. The first letter is given to help you choose. Use each word once. Some words, such as *everyone* and *everybody*, can work in more than one place. Once you've used a word, cross it off so you won't use it again.

anybody	anywhere	everyone	nobody	nothing	somewhere
anything	everybody	everywhere	no one	something	

1. Why does a surgeon wear a mask during operations?
   . . . So if *a* ____________ goes wrong, *n* ____________ can identify her.

2. If an apple a day keeps the doctor away, what does garlic do?
   . . . It keeps *e* ____________ away!

3. What runs all the time without ever getting *a* ____________ ?
   . . . your refrigerator

4. Boy: "This scale is broken."
   Girl: "How do you know that?"
   Boy: "It tells *e* ____________ a different weight."

5. What can you lose and *n* ________ else can find for you?
   . . . your temper

6. What time is it when you find King Kong in your bed?
   . . . Time to sleep *s* ____________ else!

7. What has *n* ____________ left but a nose when it loses an eye?
   . . . the word ~~*noise*~~

8. How are banks and trees alike?
   . . . They have branches *e* ____________.

9. What did one eye say to the other?
   . . . "Between you and me, *s* ____________ smells."

10. Which moves faster, heat or cold?
    . . . Heat. *A* ____________ can catch cold.

Verbs • • • • • • • • • • • Rules to Remember

Rule: **Verbs are words that show action.**

Why do pilots fly past Peter Pan's home?
. . . They see the sign that says "Never Land."

Why do dragons sleep during the day?
. . . So that they can fight knights.

Rule: **Verbs can also show existence by using forms of the verb *to be*.**

Mother: "When he grows up, I want our son to be a philanthropist."
Father: "Why?"
Mother: "Philanthropists are millionaires or billionaires."

Teacher: "If there were six flies on the table and you swatted one of them, how many would be left?"
Student: "One."
Teacher: "How do you figure that?"
Student: "Only the dead one wouldn't fly away."

Rule: **The infinitive form of a verb is expressed as the word *to* plus the verb.**

Why did the man wear three jackets to paint his bathroom?
. . . The directions said to put on three coats.

What must an alligator pay to drive over a toll bridge?
. . . a reptoll

Rule: **Present tense verbs express a fact or opinion about action happening now.**

Boy: "Why did you just swallow $1.65?!"
Girl: "Because it was my lunch money."

What falls into a puddle without rippling the water?
. . . sunshine

Directions: Choose a verb from the box to complete each joke. Each verb is used once.

hold	keep	want	make	move
is	pay	bring	hate	enjoy

1. Tourist: "How do you ________________________ your workers?"
   Rancher: "With buffalo bills."

2. Which tool is the best to ________________________ to a gold rush?
   . . . Take your pick.

3. When can an old horse ________________________ as fast as a speeding train?
   . . . when it's on the train

4. What can you put in a sandbag to ________________________ it weigh less?
   . . . a hole

5. Why do ghosts ________________________ riding in elevators?
   . . . It raises their spirits.

6. What can you ________________________ in your left hand but never in your right hand?
   . . . your right elbow

7. Why do rabbits go on strike?
   . . . They ________________________ a raise in celery.

8. How can you ________________ your hair dry in the shower?
   . . . Don't turn on the water.

9. When ________________ a car not a car?
   . . . when it turns into a driveway

10. Why do Dalmatians ________________________ baths?
    . . . They don't want to be spotless.

Commands • • • • • • • • • Rules to Remember

Rule: **In a command, the sentence begins with a verb. The subject *you* is understood.**

What did the pencil say to the pencil sharpener?
. . . "Quit going in circles and just get to the point!"

- *Explanation: this can be read as "You quit going in circles." The "you" is understood but not stated.*

What did one bee say to another?
. . . "Buzz off!"

- *Explanation: read as "You buzz off." The "you" is understood but not stated.*

What should you do if you smash your big toe?
. . . Call a tow truck.

- *Explanation: read as "You call a tow truck." The "you" is understood but not stated.*

Rule: **Commands can start with contractions.**

What did the limestone say to the geologist?
. . . "Don't take me for granite."

- *Explanation: read as "Don't you take me for granite." The "you" is understood but not stated.*

Rule: **Commands can also start with exclamations or the word *please*.**

Patient: "Doc, I've thrown out my back. What should I do?"
Doctor: "Quick! Look through your trash before it's collected."

- *Explanation: read as "You look quick..." The "you" is understood but not stated.*

What did the bowling pins say to the bowling ball?
. . . "Please spare us."

- *Explanation: read as "You please spare us." The "you" is understood but not stated.*

Commands • • • • • • • • • • • Practice Page

Directions: Fill in an appropriate verb to start each command.

1. What did the jar of mayonnaise say to the refrigerator?
   . . . ______________________ your door . . . I'm dressing!

2. What did the duck say to the waitress at the end of his meal?
   . . . "Just ______________________ it on my bill."

3. Girl: "I lost my temper yesterday."
   Boy: " ______________________ look at me. I didn't find it."

4. How do you make a witch scratch?
   . . . ______________________ away her "w"

5. What did one Tyrannosaurus Rex say to the other?
   . . . "______________________ out of my terror-tory!"

6. How can you catch a squirrel?
   . . . ______________________ up a tree and act like a nut.

7. What did one sleepy pig say to the other?
   . . . "______________________ hogging all the blankets!"

8. Girl: "This lightning scares me."
   Boy: "______________________ worry. It'll be over in a flash."

9. What did the raspberry bush say to the farmer?
   . . . "______________________ picking on me!"

10. What should you do when you feel run down?
    . . . ______________________ the license plate number of the car that ran you down.

Past Tense Verbs • • • • Rules to Remember

A past tense verb shows an action occurred in the past and has been completed.

Rule: **To form the past tense of most verbs, add the letters *ed* to the end.**

What did the judge say when a skunk wandered into her courtroom?
. . . "Odor in the court!"

- ***Explanation: "wandered" is the past tense of "wander."***

What did they name the cat after it crossed the Death Valley Desert?
. . . Sandy Claws

- ***Explanation: "crossed" is the past tense of "cross."***

Rule: **To form the past tense of verbs that end with an *e*, simply add the letter *d* to the end.**

During the rainy season, what is raised in Brazil?
. . . umbrellas

- ***Explanation: "raised" is the past tense of "raise."***

What did the ocean say to the jet that flew over?
. . . Nothing; it just waved.

- ***Explanation: "waved" is the past tense of "wave."***

Which part of the corn plant served in the army?
. . . the kernels

- ***Explanation: "served" is the past tense of "serve."***

Rule: **To form the past tense of verbs that end with a short vowel and consonant, double the consonant and add the letters *ed* to the end.**

Assistant runs into the tent shouting: "Come quickly! I've just spotted a leopard!"
Biologist: "You did not. They're born that way."

- ***Explanation: "spotted" is the past tense of "spot."***

Rule: **To form the past tense of verbs that end with a consonant + *y*, change the *y* to *i* and add the letters *ed* to the end.**

What famous musical group terrified potato plants?
. . . the Beatles

- ***Explanation: "terrified" is the past tense of "terrify."***

Past Tense Verbs • • • • • • • Practice Page

Directions: Form the past tense of the verb(s) in parentheses to complete each riddle.

1. Why was the train station ______________________ Fish Hook? (*name*)
   . . . It was at the end of the line.

2. What ______________________ after it ______________________ cats and dogs? (*happen, rain*)
   . . . Joey ______________________ in a poodle. (*step*)

3. Boy: "Which cowboys are ______________________ with their boots on? (*bury*)
   Girl: "Dead ones."

4. Girl: "When would you like me to come to your house to sing?"
   Boy: "After we've ______________________ away." (*move*)

5. Girl: "I ______________________ sleeping with my bycicle last night." (*start*)
   Boy: "Why did you do that?"
   Girl: "I was tired of sleepwalking."

6. Boy: "Save Mart is the only honest store in town."
   Girl: "Why do you think that?"
   Boy: "I lost my wallet and went into every store looking for it. Only Save Mart ______________________ it to me." (*return*)
   Girl: "How does that prove that the other stores are dishonest?"
   Boy: "All of the others ______________________ having it." (*deny*)

7. Why is the letter B ______________________ hot? (*consider*)
   . . . It makes oil boil.

8. Boy: "That's one dumb guy! He read a sign that said, "Man wanted for robbery."
   Girl: "So what?"
   Boy: "He ______________________ for the job." (*apply*)

Irregular Verbs • • • • • Rules to Remember

Rule: **Some verbs form the past tense in unusual ways. There are no real rules to explain these. They must simply be memorized.**

Why did the vampire's girlfriend break up with him?

. . . She thought he was a pain in the neck!

- *Explanation: "thought" is the past tense of "think."*

Daughter: "Did you know that George Washington once threw a silver dollar across the Potomac River?"

Father: "Yes, but you have to remember that a dollar went much farther in those days."

- *Explanation: "threw" is the past tense of "throw."*

Girl: "When you gave me this cat, you said it was good for mice. Well, he hasn't caught a single one."

Boy: "Isn't that good for mice?"

- *Explanation: "caught" is the past tense of "catch"; "said" is the past tense of "say."*

Why did the newspaper blush?

. . . It saw the comic strip.

- *Explanation: "saw" is the past tense of "see."*

What did the witch say to her broom?

. . . You swept me off my feet.

- *Explanation: "swept" is the past tense of "sweep."*

Why was the mummy so nervous?

. . . He was all wound up.

- *Explanation: "wound" is the past tense of "wind."*

Astronaut: "On my last space flight I didn't sleep for ten days."

Friend: "Weren't you exhausted?"

Astronaut: "Oh, no. I slept at night."

- *Explanation: "slept" is the past tense of "sleep."*

Boy: "My grandpa's hard of hearing, and a doctor said that she could operate to improve his hearing."

Girl: "So he's having the operation?"

Boy: "No. He said that he's 90 years old and has heard enough already."

- *Explanation: "heard" is the past tense of "hear."*

Irregular Verbs • • • • • • • • Practice Page

Directions: Fill in the irregular past tense form of each verb in parentheses to complete each joke.

1. Boy: "Did you hear that they've found bones on the moon?"
   Girl: "Oh dear. That means that the cow must not have ________________________ it." (*make*)

2. What is ______________ by the yard but worn by the foot? (*buy*)
   . . . carpeting

3. Why was the baseball player sent to jail?
   . . . They ______________ him stealing a base. (*catch*)

4. Boy: "How did you escape from the bloodhounds that were chasing you?"
   Girl: "I ________________________ a penny into the river, and they followed the cent." (*throw*)

5. Girl: "This weekend I ________________________ my arm in three places." (*break)*
   Boy: "I'd stay out of those places!"

6. Girl: "We just ________________________ back from the doctor's office. My baby brother ________________________ a foot!" (*come, grow*)
   Boy: "Gosh, I hope he grows the other one, too."

7. Girl: "I heard your dad was a conductor. Did he work for a railroad or an orchestra?"
   Boy: "Neither. Lightning ________________________ him." (*strike*)

8. Why did the student bring a ruler to bed?
   . . . She wanted to see how long she ________________________. (*sleep*)

9. Why did the weather forecaster bring soap to work?
   . . . She ________________________ there would be showers. (*think*)

10. Boy: "Was Rome ________________________ in a day?" (*build*)
    Girl: "No, silly, in Italy."

-ing Verbs • • • • • • • • • Rules to Remember

***Rule:* When the letters *ing* are added to a verb, it shows that the action is continuing over time.**

How can you stop your dog from barking in the front seat of your car?

. . . Put him in the back seat.

- *Explanation: the base verb in the sentence is "to bark."*

***Rule:* Verbs ending in *ing* can be either past, present, or future tense. You can tell when the action occurred from the helping verbs.**

What did one geologist say to the other?

. . . "Are you going to the rock festival?"

- *Explanation: the helping verb is "are," which shows intended or expected future action.*

Why did the cookies go to the doctor?

. . . They were feeling crumby.

- *Explanation: the helping verb is "were," which describes how the cookies felt at a past time.*

***Rule:* For verbs that end with a consonant + *e*, drop the *e* before adding the letters *ing* to the end.**

Police officer: "Your license says that you need glasses. Why don't you have them on?"

Driver: "I have contacts."

Officer: "Well, I don't care who you know. I'm giving you a ticket!"

- *Explanation: the base verb is "to give."*

Why did the burglar take a shower before leaving the house he had broken into?

. . . He wanted to make a clean getaway.

- *Explanation: the base verb is "to leave."*

***Rule:* For verbs that end with a short vowel and consonant, double the consonant and add the letters *ing* to the end.**

What kind of running almost always means walking?

. . . running out of gas

- *Explanation: the base verb is "to run."*

What's the difference between a river and a marathon runner?

. . . A river can run for 26 miles without ever getting out of its bed.

- *Explanation: the base verb is "to get."*

***Rule:* For the verbs *die*, *tie*, lie, etc., change the *ie* to a *y*, then add the letters *ing*.**

How do monsters keep from dying?

. . . They never leave the living room.

- *Explanation: the base verb is "to die."*

-ing Verbs • • • • • • • • • • • • Practice Page

Directions: Complete each joke by writing the continuous action form of each verb given in parentheses.

1. Why did the cat move to a new home?

   . . . His old neighborhood was ______________________ to the dogs. (*go*)

2. What do liars do after ______________________? (*die*)

   . . . lie still

3. What happened when the man gargled with gunpowder?

   . . . He kept ______________________ off his mouth. (*shoot*)

4. What did one elevator say to the other?

   . . . "I think I'm ______________________ down with something." (*come*)

5. What do you get while ______________________? (*snowboard*)

   . . . a chill thrill

6. How are spiders like tops?

   . . . They're often ______________________. (*spin*)

7. Why did the radish turn bright red?

   . . . It saw the salad ______________________. (*dress*)

8. What did the flower say to the bee?

   . . . "Quit ______________________ me!" (*bug*)

9. How is __________________ a cake like a baseball game? (make)

   . . . They both depend on the batter.

10. What runs from New York City to San Francisco without ever ______________________? (*move*)

    . . . railroad tracks

Contractions • • • • • • • • Rules to Remember

Rule: **A contraction is a short form of two words, one of which is a verb. An apostrophe replaces the missing letter(s) of the second word. For example, *there's* means "there is" or "there has."**

Woman: "Whenever I'm down in the dumps, I get some new shoes."
Friend: "So that's where you get them!"

- *Explanation: "I'm" = "I am"; " "that's" = "that is."*

Why did the cat let the genie out of the bottle?
. . . He hoped he'd be granted three fishes.

- *Explanation: "he'd" = "he would."*

Lawyer: Your uncle left you 500 clocks."
Heir: Then I guess it'll take a long time to wind up his estate, won't it?

- *Explanation: "it'll" = "it will"; "won't" = "will not."*

Son: "I cooked breakfast in my pajamas."
Mother: "I think a frying pan would've worked better."

- *Explanation: "would've" = "would have."*

Rule: **One contraction is the short form of a single word (*can't* stands for *cannot*).**

Why is it so hard to fool a snake?
. . . You can't pull its leg.

What kind of beans can't grow in any garden?
. . . jelly beans

Rule: **Sometimes a contraction is the short form of two words, the first of which is a noun's name. Although we often use this form in speech, it is rarely used in writing (unless it's conversation or informal writing, like a diary).**

Why would Snow White make a great judge?
. . . because Snow White's the fairest in the land

- *Explanation: "Snow White's" = "Snow White is."*

Why is a mouse like hay?
. . . because the cat'll eat it

- *Explanation: cattle eat hay; "cat'll" = "cat will."*

Contractions • • • • • • • • • • Practice Page

Directions: Complete each joke by writing the contraction for the word(s) in parentheses.

1. Car salesperson: "This car had just one careful owner."
   Customer: "Are you kidding me? This ____________ a wreck!" (*car is*)
   Car salesperson: "Well, the other three owners ____________ as careful." (*were not*)

2. Why ____________ the boy have told jokes while ice skating? (*should not*)
   . . . The ice ____________ cracked up. (*could have*)

3. What did one plate say to the other?
   . . . "____________________on me." (*Dinner is*)

4. Why do they show bad movies on jet planes?
   . . . because the audience ____________ get up and walk out! (*cannot*)

5. Baby's mom: "____________ 14 months old now. ____________ been walking since he was 11 months." (*He is, He has*)
   Visitor: "My goodness, he must be tired!"

6. Daughter: "Dad, will you help me to find the least common denominator?"
   Dad: " ____________ tell me they____________ found it yet; they were looking for it when I was your age!" (*Do not, have not*)

7. Boy: " ____________ going to be the first person to land on the sun!" (*I am*)
   Girl: "You ____________ do that;____________ burn up!" (*cannot, you will*)
   Boy: "No I _________ . ____________ got it all figured out: ____________ just land at night." (*will not, I have, I will*)

8. Principal: "This is the fifth time this week____________ been sent to my office. What do you have to say for yourself?!" (*you have*)
   Student: "____________ glad ____________ Friday." (*I am, it is*)

Helping Verbs • • • • • • • • Rules to Remember

***Rule:* Helping verbs "help" form verb tenses by showing past and future action.**

Diner: "Do you serve crabs?"

Waiter: "I will serve anybody, sir. Have a seat."

- ***Explanation: "do" helps "serve"; "will" helps "serve."***

***Rule:* Common helping verbs are forms of the verb "to be" (*am, is, are, was, were, been*).**

How is the moon like a dollar?

. . . Both have four quarters.

- ***Explanation: "is" helps "like."***

***Rule:* Other common helping verbs are forms of the verb "to have" (*has, had, have*).**

Why did the astronaut sneak into the ladies' room?

. . . He wanted to go where no man had gone before.

- ***Explanation: "had" helps "gone."***

***Rule:* Helping verbs also come from the verb "to do" (*do, did, does*).**

What did one car muffler say to the other?

. . . "Boy, am I exhausted!"

- ***Explanation: "did" helps "say"; "am" helps "exhausted."***

***Rule:* Also included as helping verbs are the words *will, would, can,* and *could*.**

How can you tell if a bee is on the phone?

. . . You'll get a buzzy signal.

- ***Explanation: "You'll" = "you will."***

Would you rather have a crocodile or a lion attack you?

. . . I'd rather they attack each other.

- ***Explanation: "I'd" = "I would."***

Girl: "Can you telephone from your car?"

Boy: "Of course! Who can't tell a phone from a car?"

- ***Explanation: "can't" = "cannot."***

***Rule:* Sometimes there are multiple helping verbs in one sentence.**

Why does everything cost less at a place where lions shop?

. . . The prices have been slashed.

- ***Explanation: "had been" helps "slashed."***

Girl: "Did you hear the joke about the bed?"

Boy: "No. Tell me."

Girl: "I can't. It hasn't been made up yet."

- ***Explanation: "hasn't been" helps "made."***

Helping Verbs • • • • • • • • • Practice Page

Directions: Write the helping verb(s) to complete each joke. The most common helping verbs are in the box. Some are used more than once.

am	was	has	have	would	did	could
are	were	had	will	do	can	

1. Why did George Washington stand in the boat as he crossed the Delaware River?
   . . . If he __________ sat down, they __________ __________ given him an oar.

2. Why __________ the employee fall asleep at work?
   . . . Her boss told her she __________ retire early.

3. What did the employment agent say to the unemployed vegetable?
   . . . "Don't worry. I __________ sure something __________ turnip soon."

4. Why did the light turn red?
   . . . So would you, if you __________ caught changing in the middle of the street!

5. Why did the bear tiptoe through the campground?
   . . . He __________ not want to wake up the sleeping bags.

6. What's the world's quietest game?
   . . . Bowling, because you __________ hear a pin drop.

7. Why did the farmer use a steamroller on his potato field?
   . . . He __________ raising mashed potatoes.

8. Judge: "The jury __________ found you innocent of stealing jewelry."
   Defendant: "Does that mean I __________ keep it?"

9. Girl: "Why __________ you keep a stick of dynamite in your car's glove compartment?"
   Boy: "To fix flat tires without using the jack."
   Girl: "What __________ you talking about?"
   Boy: "If I get a flat tire, I __________ just blow it up."

10. Why couldn't anyone find the deck of cards?
    . . . They __________ been lost in the shuffle.

Helping Verbs • • • • • • • • • • • • More Practice

Directions: Finish the joke by writing a helping-verb contraction from the box. The contractions may be used more than once.

'm	's	're	've	'll	'd
(am)	*(is, has)*	*(are)*	*(have)*	*(will)*	*(had, would)*

1. Boy: "Why does your mom always wear a helmet while she________ using the computer?"
   Girl: "She__________ afraid that it__________ crash."

2. First Burglar: "Oh no, it__________ the police! Quick, jump out the window!"
   Second Burglar: "But we__________ on the 13th floor!"
   First Burglar: "This is no time to be superstitious . . . just do it!"

3. Boy: "My family__________ moving to a nudist colony."
   Girl: "That__________ take all the fun out of Halloween."

4. Why should you tell ghost stories on a hot day when the air conditioning isn't working?
   . . . because they__________ chilling

5. Why did the baseball player take his bat to the library?
   . . . His teacher told him he__________ better hit the books.

6. What did the fox say when it was introduced to a chicken?
   . . . I__________ pleased to eat you.

7. Girl: "I__________ just come from the beauty parlor."
   Boy: "Too bad it was closed."

8. Boy: "I__________ afraid that I__________ going to die."
   Girl: "Nonsense. That__________ the last thing you__________ do."

9. What would happen to you if you fell on a CD?
   . . . You__________ get a slipped disc.

10. Police Officer: "I__________ writing you a ticket for driving 90 miles an hour."
    Driver: "That________ridiculous. I_________ only been driving for 15 minutes."

Adjectives • • • • • • • • • Rules to Remember

Rule: **An adjective is a word that describes a noun by giving more information about that noun.**

Why was the computer always exhausted when it got home from work?
. . . It had a hard drive.

- ***Explanation: "hard" describes "drive."***

What happens if you cross a bridge with a car?
. . . You reach the other side.

- ***Explanation: "other" describes "side."***

Why did the woman say that a room full of married couples was empty?
. . . because there wasn't a single person in it

- ***Explanation: "married" describes "couples"; "empty" describes "room"; "single" describes "person."***

Rule: **Number, order, color, and size words are frequently used as adjectives.**

What ship has no captain but two mates?
. . . friendship

- ***Explanation: "two" describes "mates."***

Who's the ringleader?
. . . the first person in a bathtub

- ***Explanation: "first" describes "person."***

Why did Ms. Tomato turn bright red?
. . . She saw Mr. Green Pea.

- ***Explanation: "bright" and "red" describes "Ms. Tomato"; "Green" describes "Pea."***

Do large ships like the *Titanic* sink very often?
. . . No, just once.

- ***Explanation: "large" describes "ships."***

Rule: **The phrase "a lot of" is often used as an adjective phrase describing a noun. "A lot" is always two separate words.**

Why is an attractive girl's face her fortune?
. . . It draws a lot of interest.

- ***Explanation: "a lot of" describes the amount of interest.***

Adjectives • • • • • • • • • • • • • Practice Page

Directions: Use the adjectives in the box to complete each joke. Each adjective is used once.

a lot of	last	many	long	bright	pink
black	sunny	ice	small	first	red

1. What stays hot, even in the refrigerator?
   . . . ______________________ peppers

2. What do you call an ______________ path along a street?
   . . . a slidewalk

3. How did the baker get wealthy?
   . . . by making ______________________ dough

4. If all the cars in this country were pink, what would we have?
   . . . a ______________________ car nation

5. Why shouldn't you add a ______________________ list of numbers on a ______________________ day?
   . . . You don't want to get sumstroke.

6. What do ants say to each other?
   . . . Nothing much; they just make ______________________ talk.

7. Why did the astronaut take a shovel on his space walk?
   . . . So he could dig a ______________________ hole.

8. Why did the teacher always wear sunglasses in school?
   . . . Her students were very ______________________.

9. How is the sun able to stay up in the sky?
   . . . It has ______________________ beams.

10. What's so unusual about money?
    . . . You have to make it ______________________ before you can make it ______________________.

Articles • • • • • • • • • • Rules to Remember

An article is a kind of adjective.

***Rule:* Use the article *the* when you are being specific or are referring to a previously mentioned person or thing or if the item is plural (more than one).**

To what kind of music did the Pilgrims dance?
. . . Plymouth Rock

Where was the Declaration of Independence signed?
. . . at the bottom

What are the true colors of the sun and the wind?
. . . The sun rose and the wind blue.

***Rule:* Use the article *a* in front of a singular noun that starts with a consonant sound or the letter *y*.**

What kind of cracker should you never put into your soup?
. . . a firecracker

What do you keep having even after giving it away?
. . . a cough

What has a foot at each end as well as a foot in the middle?
. . . a yardstick

***Rule:* Use the article *an* in front of a singular noun that starts with a vowel sound.**

What is sometimes right but never wrong?
. . . an angle

What can speak any language in the world?
. . . an echo

What do you call a cow that doesn't give milk?
. . . an udder failure

***Rule:* Use the article *an* in front of words *hour* and *honor* because the *h* is silent.**

Police officer: "I'm giving you a ticket. You just sped past a sign stating this is a 45-mile-per-hour zone."

Driver: "But how am I supposed to read the sign when I'm going 70 miles an hour?"

Articles • • • • • • • • • • • • • Practice Page

Directions: Finish each riddle by writing *a, an,* or *the.*

1. What is most useful when it's used up?
   . . . ____________ umbrella

2. What's the best year for grasshoppers?
   . . . ____________ leap year

3. What comes up to the door but never gets in?
   . . . ____________ steps

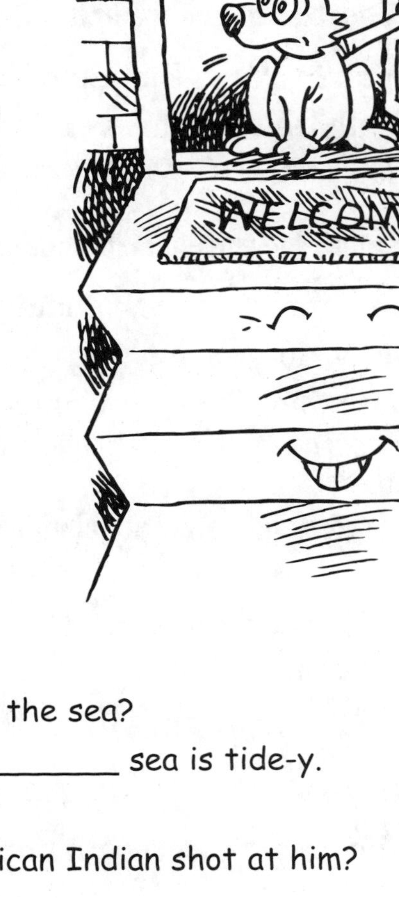

4. What has hundreds of needles but never sews?
   . . . ____________ porcupine

5. What must be broken before it's of any use?
   . . . ____________ egg

6. Which side of a rabbit has the most hair?
   . . . ____________ outside

7. What driver doesn't need a license?
   . . . ____________ screwdriver

8. What do you serve that you can't eat?
   . . . ____________ tennis ball

9. What's the difference between the land and the sea?
   . . . ____________ land is dirt-y, but ____________ sea is tide-y.

10. What happened to the Pilgrim when an American Indian shot at him?
    . . . He had ____________ arrow escape.

Comparisons • • • • • • • • Rules to Remember

Comparative adjectives compare two people, things, or ideas.

***Rule:* Comparative adjectives end with the letters *r* or *er*.**

Teacher: "Things expand from heat and contract from cold. Can you name an example?"

Student: "Sure . . . days. When it's summer, the days get longer. When it's winter, they get shorter.

- *Explanation: "long" + "er" = "longer"; "short" + "er" = "shorter."*

What's harder to catch the faster you run?

. . . your breath

- *Explanation: "hard" + "er" = "harder"; "fast" + "er" = "faster."*

***Rule:* When an adjective ends in a short vowel and consonant, the consonant is doubled before the *er* is added.**

Who's bigger, Mrs. Bigger or her child?

. . . Actually, her child is a little Bigger.

- *Explanation: "big" + "g" + "er" = "bigger."*

***Rule:* When the adjective ends in a consonant + *y*, the *y* is dropped and *ier* is added.**

Boy: "My mom's car is funnier than yours."

Girl: "Why do you say that?"

Boy: "My mom drives a Jokeswagon."

- *Explanation: "funny" + "er" = "funnier."*

***Rule:* The words *more* and *better* are comparative adjectives. Note the *r* used near the end of both words.**

Patient: "I need more of those iron pills you gave me."

Doctor: "Why?"

Patient: "I left them out in the rain, and they rusted."

Is it better to write on a full or an empty stomach?

. . . It's better to write on paper.

Comparisons • • • • • • • • • • • Practice Page

Directions: Complete each joke by writing the comparative form of the adjective given.

1. Why did the grandfather clocks strike?
   . . . They wanted ______________________ hours. (*short*)
2. What gets ______________________ the more you take away from it? (*large*)
   . . . a hole
3. Right now everyone in the world is doing exactly the same thing. What is it?
   . . . growing ______________________ (*old*)
4. Customer: "Waiter, how do you serve shrimps?"
   Waiter: "We just bend ______________________." (*low*)
5. Why did the elephant buy a ______________________ car? (*big*)
   . . . She needed more trunk space.
6. Post office clerk: "This package is too heavy. You have to put more postage on it."
   Customer: "How will that make my package ______________________?" (*light*)
7. Why couldn't the weightlifter cross the road?
   . . . The traffic was ______________________ than he could handle. (*heavy*)
8. What did the tall smokestack say to the ______________________ one? (*short*)
   . . . You're too young to smoke.
9. Teacher: "The main river in Egypt is the Nile. Can you name some of the ______________________ rivers?" (*small*)

   Student: "The juveniles?"
10. What gets ______________________ the more it dries? (*wet*)
    . . . a towel

Superlatives • • • • • • • Rules to Remember

Superlative adjectives compare three or more people, things, or ideas.

Rule: **Superlative adjectives have the ending *st* or *est* added.**

What's the loudest pet?

. . . a trumpet

- *Explanation: "loud" + "est" = "loudest" = the most loud of all pets.*

Which fruit has the shortest temper?

. . . the crab apple

- *Explanation: "short" + "est" = "shortest" = the most short of all fruits.*

Rule: **When an adjective ends in a short vowel and consonant, the consonant is doubled before the *est* is added.**

Where can you find the world's biggest spider?

. . . on the Worldwide Web

- *Explanation: "big" + "g" + "est" = "biggest" = the most big of all spiders.*

Rule: **When the adjective ends in a consonant + *y*, the *y* is changed to *i* and then *est* is added.**

Mother: "Wash your hands after you fill your piggybank. Money is one of the dirtiest things you can touch."

Son: "So that's why they call people filthy rich!"

- *Explanation: "dirty" + "est" = "dirtiest" = the most dirty of all things.*

Rule: **The words *most* and *best* are superlative adjectives. Note the *st* used near the end of both words.**

Which insect is the most religious?

. . . the praying mantis

What's the best way to double your money?

. . . fold it in half

What kind of books do skunks read?

. . . best smellers

Superlatives • • • • • • • • • • Practice Page

Directions: Complete each joke or riddle by writing the superlative form of the adjective given in parentheses.

1. What's the world's ________________________ vegetable? (*lazy*)
   . . . a couch potato
2. Boy: "How can I get to the ________________________ hospital quickly?" (*close*)
   Girl: "Go stand in the middle of that busy street."
3. What's the ________________________ waterway in the U.S.A.? (*scary*)
   . . . the Erie Canal
4. What's the ________________________ piece of classroom furniture? (*long*)
   . . . a multiplication table
5. What are the ________________________ ocean dwellers? (*strong*)
   . . . mussels
6. What professional athletes are the ________________________ eaters? (*sloppy*)
   . . . basketball players, because they dribble a lot
7. What was the ________________________ invention of all time? (*great*)
   . . . the wheel, because it got things rolling
8. What's the ________________________ way to get on TV? (*fast*)
   . . . Sit on top of your set.
9. What part of the human body is the ________________________? (*noisy*)
   . . . the ear drums
10. Which pine has the ________________________ needles? (*sharp*)
    . . . the porcupine

Compounds • • • • • • • • • Rules to Remember

Rule: Hyphenate two or more words forming a compound adjective in front of the noun they describe.

Why did the kitten take the Red Cross lifesaving course?
. . . He wanted to be a first-aid kit.

- *Explanation: The words "first" and "aid" form a compound adjective describing the noun "kit."*

Girl: "Captain Cook made three around-the-world voyages and was killed during one of them."
Boy: "Which one?"
Girl: "The last one."

- *Explanation: There are three words in this compound adjective describing the noun "voyages."*

Rule: One of the two "words" in a compound adjective may be a number.

Why was the army so tired on April 1?
. . . They had just finished a 31-day March.

- *Explanation: Both "31" and "day" form a compound adjective that describes the noun "March."*

What problem does a five-foot woman have?
. . . She needs two-and-a half pairs of shoes.

- *Explanation: "Five foot" is used as a compound adjective to describe the noun "woman."*

Rule: Compound adjectives beginning with the word *self* are always hyphenated, whether or not they are followed by a noun.

Why did the vacuum cleaner sign up for *self*-defense classes?
. . . It was tired of being pushed around.

Compounds • • • • • • • • • • • • • Practice Page

Directions: Find the compound adjectives. Some are in the riddle and others are in the answer. Put a hyphen between the words of the compound adjective. Underline the noun that follows them.

Example: Zookeeper: "The man⊖eating lion has escaped. Run for your life!"
Woman: "I'm not going to run; I have nothing to worry about"
Zookeeper: "What do you mean?"
Woman: "It's a *man*⊖eating lion, isn't it?"

1. What do you call a mouse shaped pothole?
   . . . a road dent
2. What did the silly photographer do?
   . . . She saved burnt out light bulbs to use in her darkroom.
3. What did the monster do when it lost its hand?
   . . . It bought another one at the second hand store.
4. What's a ten letter word that starts with gas?
   . . . automobile
5. What's the world's longest punctuation mark?
   . . . the 100 yard dash
6. What do you call a scared deep sea diver?
   . . . chicken of the sea
7. Why did the shopping cart have such low self esteem?
   . . . It was always getting pushed around.
8. How do you turn a pineapple into a squash?
   . . . Drop it from a third floor window.
9. How can you avoid that run down feeling?
   . . . Always look both ways before crossing a street.
10. Why did the engineer always dream about his train?
    . . . He had a one track mind.

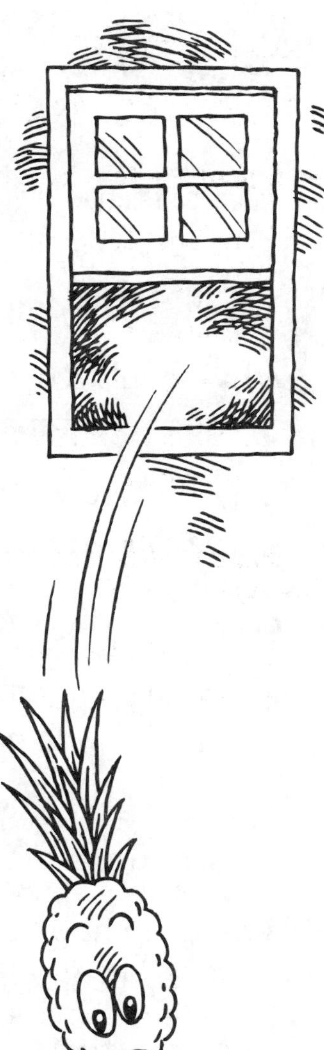

Adverbs • • • • • • • • • • Rules to Remember

Rule: **Adverbs are words that describe a verb or an adjective.**

Why don't monsters ever eat clowns?
. . . They taste funny.

- *Explanation: The adverb "funny" tells more about the verb "taste."*

What goes up without ever coming down?
. . . your age

- *Explanation: The adverb "up" tells more about the verb "goes."*

Why did the firefly fail the test?
. . . He wasn't very bright.

- *Explanation: The word "very" tells more about the verb "bright."*

Rule: **Adverbs tell how, when, where, and to what degree.**

Doctor: "You have acute appendicitis."
Patient: "I came <u>here</u> to be treated, not complimented!"

Why should you <u>never</u> tell a secret near a clock?
. . . because time will tell

Why is it so hard for a ladybug to play hide and seek?
. . . because she's <u>always</u> spotted

Rule: **Many adverbs end with the letters *ly*.**

Did George Washington ever hunt bear?
. . . No, he was always fully clothed when he went hunting.

Who deliberately drives away every customer?
. . . a taxicab driver

Why are rabbits so good at math?
. . . They really know how to multiply.

What did the magnet say to the steel?
. . . "I find you irresistibly attractive."

- *Note: The "e" at the end of the adjective "irresistible" was dropped before the "ly" was added.*

Adverbs • • • • • • • • • • • • Practice Page

Directions: Write the adverb from the box that best completes each joke. Use each word once.

ever	rarely	always	really	simply
down	truthfully	quickly	repeatedly	early

1. How can you ________________________ cool down a bath that's too hot?
   . . . Dump in a pot of chili.
2. What's the only thing you can break ____________________ by saying its name?
   . . . silence
3. Why should you hope the rain keeps up?
   . . . So it won't come ________________________.
4. Why don't Batman and Robin ________________________ go fishing together?
   . . . Robin eats all the worms.
5. What did one fly say to another?
   . . . "You ________________________ bug me."
6. What question can you never ________________________ answer yes?
   . . . Are you asleep?
7. Teacher: "What is the speed of light?"
   Student: "I don't know, but it gets here too ________________________ in the morning."
8. Where can you ________________________ find diamonds?
   . . . in a deck of cards
9. Why did the boy ____________________ kick his computer?
   . . . He wanted to boot it up.
10. Why do anteaters ________________________ become ill?
    . . . because they're full of anty bodies

Prepositions • • • • • • • • Rules to Remember

***Rule:* Prepositions link words or ideas. They include the short, but necessary, connecting words *at, to, for, in, on, of,* and *with*.**

At what time do most people go to the dentist?
. . . tooth-hurty

Did Tyrannosaurus Rex entertain often?
. . . Yes, he always had friends for dinner.

Why is no fun to play soccer with pigs?
. . . They always hog the ball.

Why didn't the mummy want to go out dancing?
. . . He was already dead on his feet.

In what course must you drop out in order to pass?
. . . skydiving

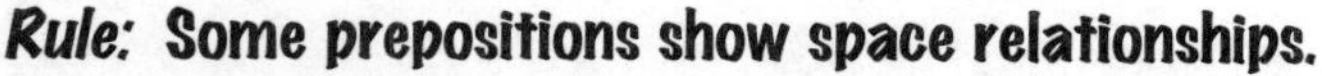

***Rule:* Some prepositions show space relationships.**

What kind of television do you find inside a haunted house?
. . . a big-scream TV

Where do books sleep?
. . . under their covers

Judge: "Why did you steal the car?"
Defendant: "It was parked in front of a cemetery, so I thought the owner was dead."

***Rule:* Some prepositions show *time relationships.* They tell when something has happened, is happening, or will happen.**

Girl: "Did you hear about the boy who met the girl in the revolving door?"
Boy: "No, what happened?"
Girl: "He's been going around with her ever since."

Father: "What did you learn during your first day of school?"
Kindergartner: "Not enough. They want me to come back tomorrow."

Why didn't the mosquitoes bother the sleeping girl?
. . . She was only annoyed after she woke up.

Prepositions • • • • • • • • • • Practice Page

Directions: Choose a preposition from the box to complete each joke. Use each preposition once.

Connecting Prepositions	Space Prepositions	Time Prepositions
with from to for	inside off around	before until after

1. Girl: "You can't park here."
   Boy: "Why not? The sign says 'Fine ______________________ Parking.'"

2. Why is opening a piano so difficult?
   . . . all of its keys are on the ______________________

3. What did the minister say right ______________________ jumping off a diving board?
   . . . "Let us spray."

4. Why was the towel bar embarrassed?
   . . . Its towel fell ______________________.

5. Why was the mama bread upset with the papa bread?
   . . . He was always loafing ______________________.

6. What animals eat ____________ their tails?
   . . . They all do. None of them can take off their tails to eat!

7. What does a farmer grow ______________________ working very hard?
   . . . extremely tired

8. Patient: "I've had two dimes stuck in my ear for three months."
   Doctor: "Why didn't you come to see me sooner?"
   Patient: "I didn't need them ________________ now."

9. How did the chemist create this new bug spray?
   . . . She started ________________ scratch.

10. What happened __________________ the tuna fish that showed up late for work?
    . . . He got canned.

Conjunctions • • • • • • • • Rules to Remember

Rule: **Coordinating conjunctions are connecting words. They join words, phrases, or clauses. Two of the most commonly used coordinating conjunctions are *and* and *or*.**

Salesman knocks on door and says to little girl in the yard: "Is your mother home?"

Little girl: "Yes."

When nobody comes to the door, the salesman says: "I thought you said she was home!"

Little girl: "She is. I don't live here."

- ***Explanation: "and" means "in addition to" or "at the same time."***

Girl: "Which do you think is more important: the sun or the moon?"

Boy: "Obviously, the moon."

Girl: "Why do you think so?"

Boy: "The moon gives us light at night, which is when we need it. The sun only gives us light during the day, which is when we don't need it."

- ***Explanation: "or" implies a choice.***

The coordinating conjunctions *but* and *yet* indicate contrast.

What has 88 teeth but never brushes them?

. . . a piano

When can a pocket be empty and yet have something in it?

. . . when it's got a hole in it

Rule: **Subordinating conjunctions, such as *so*, *unless*, and *because* indicate cause and effect.**

Why was the mummy sent into the game to pinch-hit?

. . . so he could wrap up the game

How are riddles just like pencils?

. . .They're no good unless they have a point.

Why did the boy keep on his shirt when he took a bath?

. . . because the label said wash and wear

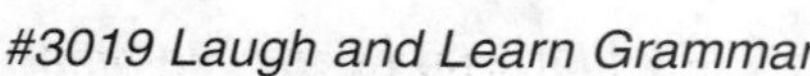

Directions: Complete each joke by writing one of the conjunctions from the box. Each conjunction is used more than once.

and	because	but	or	so

1. Teacher: "Where is the English Channel?"
   Student: "I don't know. We don't have cable, __________ we only get the local stations."

2. How do you know that the moon prefers clear nights?
   . . . __________ when the clouds disappear, the moon beams

3. What coat has no zipper __________ buttons __________ must be put on wet?
   . . . a coat of paint

4. Which are the most mathematical bugs?
   . . . Mosquitoes. They subtract from pleasure, add to misery, divide your attention, __________ multiply rapidly.

5. Mother: "Why are animal crackers spread all over the table?"
   Child: "I'm searching them."
   Mother: "For what?"
   Child: "The box says you shouldn't eat them if the seal is broken.
   . . . __________, I'm looking for the seal."

6. Girl: "How was the play you went to last night?"
   Boy: "It was good, __________ I only saw the first act."
   Girl: "Why?"
   Boy: "The program said, "Act 2. . . Three Months Later."
   . . . __________ I went home."

7. Why couldn't the mummy answer the telephone?
   . . . __________ he was tied up

8. Hopeful boyfriend: "Sir, I'd like to ask for your daughter's hand in marriage."
   Father: "Sorry, you've got to take all of her __________ nothing."

9. What occurs once in a minute, twice in a moment, __________ never in a hundred thousand years?
   . . . the letter M

10. How was the blind carpenter's sight restored?
    . . . He picked up his hammer __________ saw.

Numbers • • • • • • • • • • • Rules to Remember

Rule: **Spell out fractions and the numbers zero through nine. Use numerals for 10 and up.**

What increases its value by one-half when turned upside down?
. . . the numeral six

What do you call two spiders that just got married?
. . . newly webs

Teacher: "If you had 10 potatoes and had to share them equally among five people, how would you do it?"
Student: "I'd mash them."

Rule: **Use numerals whenever the number is an amount of money, a date, an age, a score, or any kind of measurement.**

Traveler: "Cabbie, how much will you charge to take me to the airport?"
Cabbie: "$10."
Traveler: "How much for my luggage?"
Cabbie: "There's no charge for luggage."
Traveler: "OK. You take my luggage, and I'll meet you there."

Boy: "What time is it?"
Girl: "I don't know, but it's not 5 o'clock yet."
Boy: "How do you know?"
Girl: "Because my mom said to be home by then, and I'm not home yet."

Boy: "Mom, what would you do if I got a 100 on my math test?"
Mom: "I'd faint."
Boy: "I thought so. That's why I settled for a 75."

Rule: **Spell out any number that begins a sentence.**

Teacher: "If you had five pieces of candy and Tommy asked you for one, how many pieces would you have left?"
Girl: "Five."

Rule: **Use a numeral with a word for numbers 1 million and up.**

Boy: "Did you know that China has a standing army of over 2 million soldiers?
Girl: "Wow! They must be really short of chairs in China."

Directions: Cross out the incorrect expression of the number in each joke.

Example: What has ~~eighteen~~ **18** legs and catches flies?
. . . a baseball team

1. What happened to the monster that took the **six 6** o'clock train home?
. . . He had to give it back.

2. If you cross poison ivy with a **four 4** leaf clover, what will you get?
. . . a rash of good luck

3. What resembles **one-half 1/2** of a block of cheese?
. . . the other half

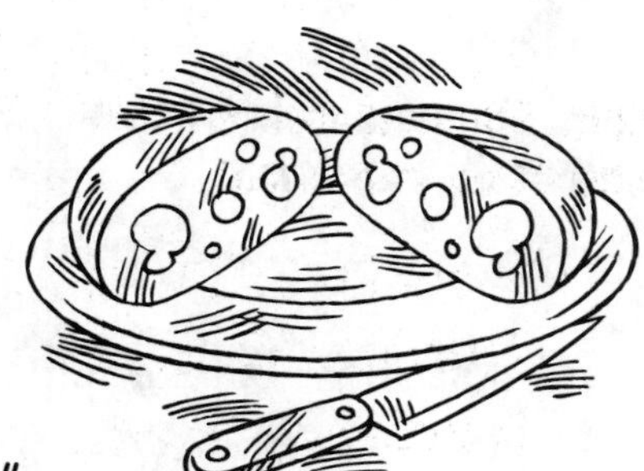

4. How can you make **seven 7** even?
. . . Take away its "s."

5. Man: "I'd hate to be **ten 10** miles up in the space shuttle."
Woman: "I'd hate to be up there without it!"

6. What comes after **nine 9**?
. . . All the rest of the numbers.

7. Teacher: "Tell the class what your book was about."
Student: "It was about **one hundred twenty-five 125** pages."

8. Why was **six 6** afraid of **seven 7**?
. . . because **seven 7** ate **nine 9**.

9. Customer: "I'd like to buy a pound of nails."
Clerk: "That'll be **four dollars $4**, plus tax."
Customer: "But I don't want any tacks, just the nails."

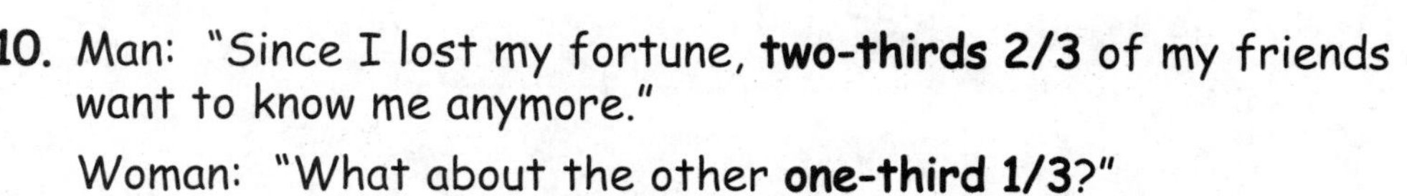

10. Man: "Since I lost my fortune, **two-thirds 2/3** of my friends don't want to know me anymore."
Woman: "What about the other **one-third 1/3**?"
Man: "They don't know that I lost it yet."

Numbers • • • • • • • • • • • • • • More Practice

Directions: Cross out the incorrect expression of the number in each joke.

Example: Why did the golfer wear **two** ~~2~~ pairs of pants?
. . . in case she got a hole in ~~1~~ **one**

1. Pet store clerk: "Why would you want to buy **five hundred 500** cockroaches?"
   Tenant: "I'm moving, and the landlord insists that I leave the apartment exactly the same as when I arrived."

2. Father: "Why did you come home at **three 3** a.m.?!"
   Son: "You told me to come home early."

3. Why couldn't the **seven 7** and the **ten 10** get married?
   . . . They were under **eighteen 18**.

4. Husband: "I've been cooking for **eleven 11** years."
   Wife: "Then I hope that dinner is ready by now."

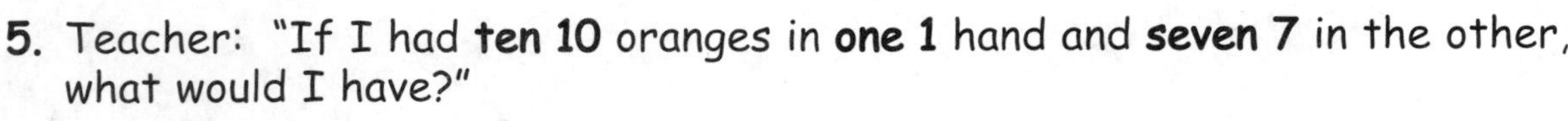

5. Teacher: "If I had **ten 10** oranges in **one 1** hand and **seven 7** in the other, what would I have?"
   Student: "Incredibly big hands."

6. Police officer: "When you went past me just now, I could tell you were pushing at least **sixty 60**."
   Woman: "How rude! I'm only **forty-five 45**."

7. What did **one 1** squirrel say to the other?
   . . . "I'm nuts about you!"

8. Teacher: "Name **six 6** wild animals."
   Student: "**Four 4** lions and **two 2** tigers."

9. Boy: "My grandpa lived to be **eighty-five 85** and never needed glasses."
   Girl: "So what? Plenty of people drink straight from the bottle."

10. Teacher: "Due to your absences, you missed **three 3** tests last week."
    Student: "I may not have taken the tests, but I didn't miss them a bit."

Question Words • • • • • • Rules To Remember

Rule: **When certain words begin a sentence, you can be pretty sure that it's a question. The main "question words" are *who, what, when, where, why, which,* and *how.***

Who performs operations at a fish hospital?

. . . the head sturgeon

- ***Explanation:** "Who" answers the question "Which person or living creature?"*

What happened to the owl with the sore throat?

. . . She stopped giving a hoot.

- ***Explanation:** "What" answers the question "Which living or nonliving thing?"*

When is a department store like a boat?

. . . when it has sales

- ***Explanation:** "When" answers the question "At which time or on which occasion?"*

Boy: "Where did you learn how to swim?"

Girl: "In the water."

- ***Explanation:** "Where" answers the question "At which location?"*

Why did the man go out on the road in a severe thunderstorm?

. . . His car needed shocks.

- ***Explanation:** "Why" answers the question "For what reason?"*

Which is the left side of a pumpkin pie?

. . . the side you haven't eaten yet

- ***Explanation:** For "which" questions, the answer requires a choice between two or more things.*

How can you tell if a jackhammer tells good jokes?

. . . if the cement is cracking up

- ***Explanation:** "How" explains the way in which something is done.*

Question Words • • • • • • • • • Practice Page

Directions: Fill in the appropriate question word to make each joke make sense. Some of the words in the box are used more than once.

Who	What	When	Where	Why	Which	How

1. ______________________ will a net hold water?

   . . . when the water turns to ice

2. ______________________ player on a little-league baseball team can hold the most milk?

   . . . the pitcher

3. ______________________ do bats go to get an education?

   . . . to night school

4. ______________________ do pigs want to be when they grow up?

   . . . ham radio operators

5. ______________________ was the math student so bad at decimals?

   . . . She just didn't get the point.

6. ______________________ can you find a spider on the Internet?

   . . . Go to its Web site.

7. ______________________ does a horse talk on the phone?

   . . . whinny he wants to

8. ______________________ is the world's strongest woman?

   . . . a policewoman, because she can hold up as many cars as she wants with one hand

9. ______________________ kind of a hawk chooses new team players?

   . . . a talon scout

10. ______________________ did the pig feel after the earthquake?

    . . . like shaken bacon.

Homophones • • • • • • • • Rules to Remember

Homophones are two (or more) words that sound alike but have different meanings. They are one of the reasons that jokes and riddles are funny. The English language is full of such humor because it has more homophones than any other currently spoken language.

Rule: **To determine which word to use, you must first determine how it's used in a sentence.**

Why did the boy stop attending barber school?
. . . They threw him out for cutting a class.

- *Explanation: "threw" is a verb, the past tense of "throw."*

Girl: "Did Sheriff Garrett shoot Billy the Kid in the end?"
Boy: "No, through his heart."

- *Explanation: "through" is an adverb describing movement.*

Why did the cat scratch a hole in the carpeting?
. . . It wanted to see the floor show.

- *Explanation: "hole" is a noun.*

From what can you take the whole away and still have some left?
. . . the word "wholesome"

- *Explanation: "whole" is an adjective that means "all."*

Boy: "May I use your phone to make a call?"
Girl: "Well, I don't know what else you could use it for."

- *Explanation: "know" is a verb.*

Father: "Look in this cage. There's a 10-foot snake in it."
Son: "Don't be ridiculous. There's no such thing as a snake with feet."

- *Explanation: "no" is an adjective or adverb meaning "not at all" or "not any."*

Why are twin witches so hard to tell apart?
. . . You can never tell which witch is which!

- *Explanation: "which" is a pronoun; "witch" is a noun.*

Teacher: "If apples are two for a dollar, how many can you buy with 50 cents?"
Student: "None. "If I had 50 cents, I'd buy a candy bar instead of an apple."

- *Explanation: "buy" is a verb.*

How did the doe win the deer marathon?
. . . by passing the buck

- *Explanation: "by" is a preposition.*

Directions: Circle the correct form of the word to complete each joke or riddle.

1. Girl: "Why do bees hum?"
   Boy: "They don't **no know** the words."

2. Diner: "Why is my bread full of **wholes holes**?
   Waitress: "What did you expect? It's **whole hole** wheat bread."

3. What did the **which witch** teach her students?
   . . . spelling

4. What kind of coach has **no know** wheels?
   . . . a sports coach

5. How much dirt is in a hole 6 feet long **by buy** 13 feet wide?
   . . . None, a **whole hole** is empty!

6. Why does the monster **by buy** the newspaper daily?
   . . . He wants to read his horror-scope.

7. If you **threw through** a blue shoe into the Red Sea, what would it become?
   . . . wet, of course

8. When does a cowboy decide **which witch** pair of boots he'll wear?
   . . . on the spur of the moment

9. Boy: "Dad, can I go to the movies?"
   Dad: "With that **hole whole** in your pants?"
   Boy: "No, with the kid next door."

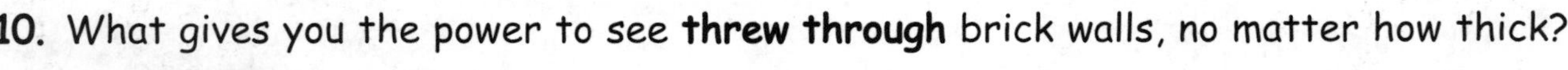

10. What gives you the power to see **threw through** brick walls, no matter how thick?
    . . . a window

They're/Their/There • • • Rules to Remember

The easiest way to learn which of these words to use is to memorize when to use **they're** and **their**. Then you know that you must use **there** in every other case.

Rule: **The word *they're* is always a contraction. Use it only when you can substitute *they are.***

Why don't frogs live very long?
. . . because they're always croaking

Father: "What are your grades like this term?"
Son: "They're underwater."
Father: "What does that mean?"
Son: "Below C level."

Why don't elephants like computers?
. . . They're afraid of the mouse.

Rule: **The word *their* is always a pronoun. Use it to show ownership.**

Why are male deer always smiling?
. . . to show off their buck teeth

Why did they open the first drive-through restaurant?
. . . so people could curb their appetites

Why were the elephants thrown out of the water park?
. . . They couldn't keep their trunks up.

Rule: **The word *there* is used as an adverb or pronoun. It is used to show a place or a position, to tell of the existence of something, or when the verb comes before the subject in a sentence.**

Boy: "That bank won't let my dad withdraw any money."
Girl: "Why not?"
Boy: "He doesn't have any in there."

- *Explanation: "there" shows place in this example.*

Girl: "What caused your flat tire?"
Boy: "There was a fork in the road."

- *Explanation: "there" shows existence in this example.*

Boy: "Why did you laugh when the teacher asked you what W-A-L-R-U-S spells?"
Girl: "Because there is no such thing as a walrus that spells."

- *Explanation: the verb "is" comes before the subject "thing."*

They're/Their/There • • • • • • Practice Page

Directions: Finish each punchline by writing *they're, their,* or *there.* Remember to capitalize the first word in a sentence.

1. How do you know that grandfather clocks are shy?
   . . . They always have ________________ hands over __________________ faces.

2. Why do people consider flowers lazy?
   . . . ______________________ always in beds.

3. What kind of animals are the easiest to weigh?
   . . . Reptiles; they always carry around ______________________ scales.

4. What's the longest word in the English language?
   . . . "Smiles"; ______________________ is a mile between the first and last letters.

5. Why do the numbers one through twelve make the best guards?
   . . . because they spend all of ______________________ time on the watch

6. If six copycats sat on a fence and one jumped down, how many would be left on the fence?
   . . . None, ______________________ all copycats!

7. Do doctors get a big charge out of their work?
   . . . No, but ______________________ patients surely do!

8. Why is winter the best time to purchase a thermometer?
   . . . because in summer ______________________ higher

9. Why were the baby strawberries upset?
   . . . ______________________ parents were in a jam.

10. When does it rain money?
    . . . whenever ______________________ is change in the weather

They're/Their/There • • • • • More Practice

Directions: Complete each joke by writing *they're, their,* or *there.* Remember to capitalize the first word in a sentence.

1. How can you tell when a spider is lying?
   . . . if it says ____________ are no strings attached

2. Where do football players buy ____________ team shirts?
   . . . in New Jersey

3. What happens when tires get old?
   . . . ____________ retired.

4. Why should you never tell a secret inside a bank?
   . . . because ____________ is always at least one teller

5. Diner: "I'm in a big hurry! Will my pancakes be long?"
   Waitress: "No, sir, ____________ round."

6. Student: "I wish I lived in ancient times."
   Teacher: "Why?"
   Student: "____________ would be a lot less history to learn."

7. Why won't witches ride brooms when angry?
   . . . ____________ afraid of flying off the handle.

8. Why is it hard to give a speech if ____________ is a goat nearby?
   . . . It'll keep butting in.

9. Why were the tennis players in the dark?
   . . . They'd lost all ____________ matches.

10. Why do frogs have terrible table manners?
    . . . While ____________ eating, they always
    stick out____________ tongues.

Its/It's • • • • • • • • • • • • • • Rules to Remember

> Choose to memorize one of the rules for **its** and **it's**. That way you'll know to use the other form whenever the rule doesn't apply.

Rule: **The word *its* is always a pronoun. Use it to show ownership.**

How can you tell where a train has gone?
. . . It leaves its tracks behind.

What did the digital watch say to its mother?
. . . Look, Mom, no hands!

Why did the dog bite its tail?
. . . to make ends meet

Rule: **The word *it's* is always a contraction. Use it only when you can substitute *it is* or *it has*.**

What gets longer at the same time that it's growing shorter?
. . . your life

- ***Explanation:*** *In this case, "it's" stands for "it is."*

How is the math equation "2 + 2 = 5" like your left leg?
. . . It's not right.

- ***Explanation:*** *In this case, "it's" stands for "it is."*

When is a watermelon like squash?
. . . when it's been run over by a tractor

- ***Explanation:*** *In this case, "it's" stands for "it has."*

Its/It's • • • • • • • • • • • • • Practice Page

Directions: Finish each joke by writing *its* or *it's*. Remember to capitalize the word if it is the first in a sentence.

1. What did the beaver say to the tree?
   . . . "____________ been nice gnawing you."
2. Why was the cornstalk furious with the farmer?
   . . . The farmer kept pulling off ____________ ears.
3. How is a window in a roof like the sun?
   . . . ____________ a skylight.
4. When is a piece of wood like a queen?
   . . . when ____________ a ruler
5. What did the horse say after eating all of ____________ hay?
   . . . "Well, that's the last straw!"
6. What kind of clothing lasts the longest?
   . . . underwear, because ____________ never worn out
7. Boy: "This is a dogwood tree."
   Girl: "How do you know?"
   Boy: "By ____________ bark."
8. What does an envelope say when ____________ licked?
   . . . Nothing; it just shuts up.
9. What's as big as a dinosaur but weighs nothing?
   . . . ____________ shadow
10. When is a door not a door?
    . . . when ____________ ajar

Its/It's • • • • • • • • • • • • • • • More Practice

Directions: Finish each joke by writing *its* or *it's*.

1. Why was the dresser embarrassed?
   . . . ____________ drawers fell down.

2. What happens to an air conditioner after ____________ been turned off?
   . . . It loses ____________ cool.

3. When is a boat like snow?
   . . . when ____________ adrift

4. What holds up a stagecoach?
   . . . ____________ wheels

5. Why is the weather forecast like a baby?
   . . . because ____________ often changed

6. How do you make an orange giggle?
   . . . Tickle ____________ navel.

7. Which bug is the best baseball fielder?
   . . . ____________ the spider, because ____________ good at catching flies.

8. How did the computer get out of jail?
   . . . It used ____________ escape key.

9. How can you turn a watch into a stopwatch?
   . . . Remove ____________ battery.

10. When is a pig like ink?
    . . . when ____________ in a pen

Your/You're • • • • • • • • • Rules to Remember

Choose to memorize one of the rules for **your** and **you're**. That way you'll know to use the other form whenever the rule doesn't apply.

Rule: **The word *your* is always a pronoun. Use it to show ownership.**

What tree do you carry in your hand?
. . . a palm

Teacher: "This homework looks like your father's handwriting!"
Student: "That's just because I used his pen."

Mother: "Wash your hands. The piano teacher is coming in 10 minutes."
Child: "Don't worry, Mom. I'll only play the black keys."

School nurse: "May I take your temperature?"
Student: "Why? Don't you have one of your own?"

Rule: **The word *you're* is always a contraction. Use it only when you can substitute *you are*.**

What should you do if you're walking across the savannah and see a lioness?
. . . Hope she doesn't see you!

What did the sink say to the dirty dishes soaking in it?
. . . "Now you're in hot water."

What's the best thing to do if you're chased by a shark?
. . . feed it jawbreakers

Your/You're • • • • • • • • • • Practice Page

Directions: Finish each punchline by writing *your* or *you're.* Remember to capitalize the first word in a sentence.

1. No matter how smart you are, what will you always overlook?
   . . . ____________ nose

2. What did Abraham Lincoln's father say when he saw young Abe's report card?
   . . . "Looks like ____________ going down in history, son."

3. When is it bad luck for a black cat to follow you?
   . . . when ____________ a mouse

4. What can you hold without ever touching it?
   . . . ____________ breath

5. Girl: "Can you carry a tune?"
   Boy: "Sure I can."
   Girl: "Then carry the one ____________ singing out in the backyard and bury it."

6. Father: "Have you done ________________ homework yet?"
   Daughter: "No; I can't figure it out. Would you please do it for me?
   Father: "No. It wouldn't be right."
   Daughter: "Well, could you give it a try anyhow?"

7. When should you wear a swimsuit to go horseback riding?
   . . . when ____________ riding on a sea horse

8. Boy: "Dad, where's the Big Dipper?"
   Dad: "Ask ____________ mother; she just unloaded the dishwasher."

9. Why does the ocean roar?
   . . . You would, too, if you had lobsters in ____________ bed.

10. Mom: "If ____________ a good boy today, I'll give you this shiny new dime."
    Son: "I'd rather have a dented old quarter."

Your/You're • • • • • • • • • • More Practice

Directions: Finish each joke by writing *your* or *you're.* Remember to capitalize it if the word starts a sentence.

---

1. Police officer: "Does ____________ dog have a license?"
   Person: "No. He's not old enough to drive."

2. When is fishing a bad way to relax?
   . . . when ____________ the worm

3. Doctor: "____________ suffering from arthritis."
   Patient: "Of course I am. What else can I do with it?"

4. How do you talk to a giraffe?
   . . . You must raise ____________ voice.

5. What did the computer keyboard say to the typist?
   . . . "____________ really pushing my buttons."

6. Girl: "I fell over 50 feet this morning."
   Boy: "Then how come ____________ not injured?"
   Girl: "It happened on a crowded school bus."

7. Robber: "____________ money or ____________ life."
   Woman: "You'd better take my life. I'll need my money for my old age."

8. Husband: "I'll make dinner. I have guests dropping over."
   Wife: "They will once they eat ____________ dinner."

9. Man: "I really benefited from ____________ treatment."
   Doctor: "But ____________ not my patient."
   Man: "No, but my Uncle Harry was, and I got his money when he died."

10. Piano teacher to mother: "____________ child plays the piano like lightning."
    Mother: "You mean she's learning fast?"
    Piano teacher: "No, I mean that she never strikes the same place twice."

Too/To/Two • • • • • • • • • Rules to Remember

The easiest way to learn which word to use is to memorize when to use **two** and **too**. Then you know that you must use **to** in every other case.

***Rule:* Use *two* for a number.**

What happens if two toads try to catch the same bug at the same time?

. . . They get tongue-tied!

What did one raindrop say to the other?

. . . Two is company, but three's a cloud.

What are the only two things you can never have for breakfast?

. . . lunch and dinner

***Rule:* Use *too* when you mean "more than enough," "extremely," or "excessively."**

What happens during a big flood?

. . . a river gets too big for its bridges

What kind of key is too large for your pocket?

. . . a donkey

Boy Melon: "Will you run away and marry me?"
Girl Melon: "We're too young; we cantaloupe!"

***Rule:* Use *too* when you can substitute the word *also*.**

Camper: "Doctor, that ointment you gave me makes my arm smart."
Doctor: "Then you'd better rub some on your head, too."

Father: "Why is your little sister crying?"
Son: "I wouldn't share my piece of cherry pie with her."
Father: "What happened to her piece?"
Son: "She cried when I ate that, too."

***Rule:* Use *to* in all other cases.**

How do bees get to school?

. . . They take the buzz.

Why did the girl go to the reptile house on the zoo's opening day?

. . . She wanted a snake preview.

Too/To/Two • • • • • • • • • • Practice Page

Directions: Complete each joke by writing *to, too,* or *two.*

1. What do you call it when a father gives 25 cents each to his son and his daughter?
   . . . a quarter to ____________

2. How did Ben Franklin feel when lightning hit the key attached to his kite?
   . . . Nothing . . . because he was ____________ shocked.

3. What time is it when the clock strikes thirteen?
   . . . time ____________ fix the clock

4. How many sides does a box always have?
   . . . ____________ — an inside and an outside

5. Why does a cowboy ride a horse?
   . . . because it's ____________ heavy to carry

6. What's the difference between electricity and lightning?
   . . . Both charge you, but you only have ____________ pay for electricity.

7. What's the best way to make fire using ____________ sticks?
   . . . Be sure one of them is a match!

8. Boy: "When you had the flu, did you run a fever, ____________?"
   Girl: "No, I just stayed in bed with it."

9. Girl: "If it took five men six hours to build a wall, how long would it take ten men to do it?"
   Boy: "But they don't need ____________ do it; the five men just did it."

10. Boy: "Your friend tried ____________ make a fool out of me."
    Girl: "Wasn't she ____________ late?"

Too/To/Two • • • • • • • • • • More Practice

Directions: Complete each joke by writing *to, too,* or *two.*

1. Why did the lake dislike the pond?
   . . . It thought the pond was ____________ shallow.

2. Daughter: "Mom, would like you ____________ fix dinner."
   Dad: "Why, is it broken?"

3. Son: "Guess what! I got a 100 in school today in ____________ subjects!"
   Father: "Wow! How did you do that?"
   Son: "I got a 50 in math and another 50 in science."

4. Why did the rooster refuse to bungee jump?
   . . . He was just ____________ chicken.

5. Son: "I studied science for ____________ hours last night and still failed today's exam."
   Mother: "Why?"
   Son: "It was a social studies test."

6. Why did the man take his computer ____________ a health clinic?
   . . . He'd been told that it had a virus.

7. Why did the sheet music try ____________ escape from the singer?
   . . . because she hit every note

8. Grandma to Joey: "If you wash your hands, I'll give you a cookie. If you wash your face, ____________, you'll get ____________ cookies."
   Joey: "Maybe I'd better take a bath!"

9. What did the blanket say ____________ the outlaw?
   . . . "Don't move. I've got you covered."

10. Attorney: "Why are you in prison?"
    Man: "I was driving ____________ slowly."
    Attorney: "Don't you mean too fast?"
    Man: "No, ____________ slowly—the police caught up with me."

Homophones • • • • • • • • • • Mixed Practice

Directions: Write the correct form of each word to complete the joke. Remember to capitalize the first word in a sentence.

its	to	two	they're	your
it's	too	there	their	you're

1. Boy: "Did you know that ____________ extremely hard ____________ get a job as a sword swallower?"
   Girl: "No. Why?"
   Boy: "____________ is cutthroat competition."

2. What did the earthquake say to the ground?
   . . . "____________ ____________ fault, not mine!"

3. Why are elephants so wrinkly?
   . . . ____________ ____________ large ____________ fit on ironing boards.

4. Teacher to parent: "I want ____________ discuss ____________ son's appearance."
   Parent: "What's wrong with his appearance?"
   Teacher: "____________ just that he hasn't made one in this classroom in a month."

5. Diner: "Waitress, ____________ is a fly in my soup!"
   Waitress: "Don't worry; ____________ complimentary. We didn't charge for it."

6. Why do banks refuse ____________ let kangaroos open checking accounts?
   . . . ____________ checks always bounce.

7. What makes a horse so unusual?
   . . . because it eats best when ____________ isn't a bit in ____________ mouth

8. What do penguins wear ____________ keep ____________ heads warm?
   . . . a polar ice cap

Than/Then • • • • • • • • • • Rules to Remember

Rule: **Use the word *than* to show a comparison.**

What do you have to know in order to teach your dogs tricks?
. . . more than the dog

What's more amazing than a dog that can count?
. . . a spelling bee

Rule: **Use the word *then* when you can substitute the words "in that case."**

Customer: "Is it customary to tip a waiter in this restaurant?"
Waiter: "It certainly is."
Customer: "Then you'd better tip me. I've been waiting for my dinner for an hour."

Patient: "I have near-constant ringing in my ears."
Doctor: "Then get an unlisted ear."

Rule: **Use the word *then* to show time sequence:**

What did the portrait say to the wall?
. . . "First they framed me and then they hung me!"

Teacher: "Oxygen was discovered in 1774."
Student: "So what did people breathe before then?"

Than/Then • • • • • • • • • • • • Practice Page

Directions: Write the word *then* or *than* to complete each joke. Remember to capitalize the first word in a sentence.

1. When is it better to give ____________ to receive?

   . . . in a snowball fight

2. Why did the girl put her sleeping bag into the fireplace and ____________ climb in?

   . . . She wanted to sleep like a log.

3. Boy: "Do you have holes in your socks?"
   Girl: "No, these are brand new."
   Boy: "____________ how did you get your feet into them?"

4. Customer: "The safety matches you sold me won't light."
   Shopkeeper: "Well, you can't get matches much safer ____________ that."

5. What breed of dog can jump higher ____________ a building?

   . . . any breed of dog . . . no building can jump!

6. Teacher: "At your age, I could name all of the U.S. presidents in the right order."
   Student: "Well sure, because back ____________ there were only about five of them."

7. Boy visiting FBI office: "Are those really photos of America's Most Wanted?"
   FBI agent: "Yes indeed."
   Boy: "____________ why didn't you keep them after you took their pictures?"

8. What did one math book say to the other?

   . . . "I've got more problems ____________ you do."

9. Boy: "Country people are much smarter ____________ city people."
   Girl: "How can you say that?!"
   Boy: "Because the population is so much denser in the city."

10. Boy: "My older brother works with more ____________ 200 people beneath him."
    Girl: "He must have a really important job. What does he do?"
    Boy: "He mows the grass in a cemetery."

Problem Verbs • • • • • • Rules to Remember

***Rule:* The verb *set* means "to place"; the verb *sit* means "to physically lower oneself into a seated position." The word *sitting* also refers to something that's already been placed.**

Why did the cowboy set his sleeping bag on the edge of a steep cliff?
. . . so he could drop off to sleep

Boy to girl as they enter the movie theater: "How far down do you want to sit?"
Girl: "All the way, of course!"

***Rule:* Use the verb "to raise" when the person or thing needs to be taken care of or physically lifted. Use the verb "to rise" when the person or thing lifts itself.**

What is a sure way to grow fat?
. . . raise pigs

- *Explanation: The pigs need to be taken care of.*

Why is tennis such a loud game?
. . . Each player raises a racket.

- *Explanation: The racket is lifted.*

Do fish bite best with the rising sun?
. . . No, they bite best with worms.

- *Explanation: The sun lifts itself.*

***Rule:* The verb "to lay" means "to place or set down." The verb "to lie" means "to recline or rest or to be untruthful." You *lay* something down. But once you've done that, then it is *lying*.**

Why do hens lay eggs?
. . . because if they dropped them, they would break

Diner: "What's wrong with these eggs that I ordered?"
Waiter: "Don't ask me. I only laid the table."

- *Explanation: "laid" is the past tense of "lay"; here it means "placed the silverware and plates."*

What lies shivering on the bottom of the ocean?
. . . a nervous wreck

What do you call a cow that's lying on the grass?
. . . ground beef

Problem Verbs • • • • • • • • • Practice Page

Directions: Complete each joke by writing the appropriate verb from the box.

setting	sit	raise	rise	lay	lying
sat	sitting	raised	rising	lays	lie

1. What's the best way to ______________________ guinea pigs?

   . . . Pick them up.

2. Why does the Statue of Liberty stand in the New York Harbor?

   . . . because it can't ______________________ down

3. When the banana couldn't sleep, why did it ______________________ still without making a sound?

   . . . It didn't want to wake the rest of the bunch.

4. Boy: "Why are you ______________________ on that clock?"

   Girl: "I want to be on time."

5. If a rooster ______________________ an egg at the peak of a slanted roof, on which side will it always fall?

   . . . neither side, because roosters don't ______________________ eggs!

6. What's dangerous about the sun ____________________ and the sun ____________________ ?

   . . . At these times, the day breaks and the night falls.

7. Why did your sister eat yeast and floor wax for breakfast?

   . . . because she wanted to ______________________ and shine

8. Why should you never believe what a person in a bed says?

   . . . because the person is ______________________

9. Patient: "Doc, I feel like I'm on pins and needles."

   Doctor: "Oops! You must have ______________________ on my knitting."

10. Two men went hunting. The first hunter ______________________ his rifle to shoot a goose.

    Friend: "Wait! That rifle isn't loaded."

    First hunter: "But the bird will be gone if I take the time to load!"

Answer Key

Note: When multiple answers are required, they are separated by commas. When multiple words could work for one answer blank, they are separated by slashes.

Page 5

1. letter
2. driver
3. dress
4. snow, rain
5. homework/ assignment
6. ticket
7. man/boy/guy
8. doctor/mom
9. neighborhood/ area/home
10. States

Page 7

1. Lake
2. Thanksgiving
3. Internet
4. Italian
5. February
6. North Pole
7. Wednesday
8. Dead
9. Santa Claus/ Christmas
10. CD

Page 8

1. Cinderella
2. Noah
3. January, February
4. Humpty Dumpty
5. Antarctica
6. Alaska
7. Mississippi
8. Mexican
9. ATM
10. Empire

Page 10

1. horns
2. stories
3. wolves
4. patches
5. letters
6. uncles, ants
7. cities, buildings, forests, trees, rivers
8. fairies
9. witches
10. rhinoceroses

Page 12

1. fish
2. feet
3. people
4. teeth
5. children
6. geese
7. deer, deer
8. cavemen
9. women
10. mice

Page 14

1. Paul Revere's
2. chickens'
3. girl's
4. vampire's
5. teenagers'
6. Jamie's
7. lions'
8. fisherman's
9. world's
10. else's

Page 16

1. They, them
2. It
3. She
4. He, him
5. I, I
6. we
7. I, I/we
8. me
9. us
10. He

Page 18

1. its
2. their
3. my
4. our
5. your
6. their
7. his
8. mine
9. her
10. your

Page 20

1. itself
2. yourself
3. herself
4. myself
5. themselves
6. himself
7. itself
8. ourselves

Page 22

1. anything, no one/ nobody
2. everyone/ everybody
3. anywhere
4. everyone/ everybody
5. no one/nobody
6. somewhere
7. nothing
8. everywhere
9. something
10. Anybody

Page 24

1. pay
2. bring
3. move
4. make
5. enjoy
6. hold
7. want
8. keep
9. is
10. hate

Page 26

1. Shut/Close
2. put
3. Don't
4. Take
5. Stay/Get
6. Climb
7. Stop/Quit
8. Don't
9. Stop/Quit
10. Get

Page 28

1. named
2. happened, rained, stepped
3. buried
4. moved
5. started
6. returned, denied
7. considered
8. applied

Answer Key (cont.)

Page 30
1. made
2. bought
3. caught
4. threw
5. broke
6. came, grew
7. struck
8. slept
9. thought
10. built

Page 32
1. going
2. dying
3. shooting
4. coming
5. snowboarding
6. spinning
7. dressing
8. bugging
9. making
10. moving

Page 34
1. car's, weren't
2. shouldn't, could've
3. Dinner's
4. can't
5. He's, He's
6. Don't, haven't
7. I'm, can't, you'll, won't, I've, I'll
8. you've, I'm, it's

Page 36
1. had, would, have
2. did, could
3. am, will
4. were
5. did
6. can
7. was
8. has, can
9. do, are, will/can
10. had

Page 37
1. she's, She's, it'll
2. it's, we're
3. family's, That'll
4. they're
5. he'd
6. I'm
7. I've
8. I'm, I'm, That's, you'll
9. You'd
10. I'm, That's, I've

Page 39
1. red
2. icy
3. a lot of
4. pink
5. long, sunny
6. small
7. black
8. bright
9. many
10. first, last

Page 41
1. an
2. a
3. the
4. a
5. an
6. the
7. a
8. a
9. The, the
10. an

Page 43
1. shorter
2. larger
3. older
4. lower
5. bigger
6. lighter
7. heavier
8. shorter
9. smaller
10. wetter

Page 45
1. laziest
2. closest
3. scariest
4. longest
5. strongest
6. sloppiest
7. greatest
8. fastest
9. noisiest
10. sharpest

Page 47
1. mouse-shaped
2. burnt-out
3. second-hand
4. ten-letter
5. 100-yard
6. deep-sea
7. self-esteem
8. third-floor
9. run-down
10. one-track

Page 49
1. quickly
2. simply
3. down
4. ever
5. really
6. truthfully
7. early
8. always
9. repeatedly
10. rarely

Page 51
1. for
2. inside
3. before
4. off
5. around
6. with
7. after
8. until
9. from
10. to

Page 53
1. so
2. because
3. or, and
4. and
5. So
6. but, so
7. because
8. or
9. but
10. and

Page 55
1. 6
2. four
3. one-half
4. seven
5. 10
6. nine
7. 125
8. six, seven, seven, nine
9. $4
10. two-thirds, one-third

Page 56
1. 500
2. 3
3. seven, 10, 18
4. 11
5. 10, one, seven
6. 60, 45
7. one
8. six, four, two
9. 85
10. three

Answer Key (cont.)

Page 58
1. When
2. Which
3. Where
4. What
5. Why
6. How
7. When
8. Who
9. What
10. How

Page 60
1. know
2. holes, whole
3. witch
4. no
5. by, hole
6. buy
7. threw
8. which
9. hole
10. through

Page 62
1. their, their
2. They're
3. their
4. There
5. their
6. they're
7. their
8. they're
9. Their
10. there

Page 63
1. there
2. their
3. They're
4. there
5. they're
6. There
7. They're
8. there
9. their
10. they're, their

Page 65
1. It's
2. its
3. It's
4. it's
5. its
6. it's
7. its
8. it's
9. its
10. it's

Page 66
1. Its
2. it's
3. it's
4. its
5. it's
6. its
7. It's, it's
8. its
9. its
10. it's

Page 68
1. your
2. you're
3. you're
4. your
5. you're
6. your
7. you're
8. your
9. your
10. you're

Page 69
1. your
2. you're
3. You're
4. your
5. You're
6. you're
7. Your, your
8. your
9. your, you're
10. Your

Page 71
1. two
2. too
3. to
4. two
5. too
6. to
7. two
8. too
9. to
10. to, too

Page 72
1. too
2. to
3. two
4. too
5. two
6. to
7. to
8. two
9. to
10. too, too

Page 73
1. it's, to, There
2. It's, your
3. They're, too, to
4. to, your, It's
5. there, it's
6. to, Their
7. there, its
8. to, their

Page 75
1. than
2. then
3. Then
4. than
5. than
6. then
7. Then
8. than
9. than
10. than

Page 77
1. raise
2. lay
3. lie
4. sitting
5. lays, lay
6. rising, setting
7. rise
8. lying
9. sat
10. raised